The Church Year

The Church Year

THE CHURCH OF ST. JOHN THE EVANGELIST
Montréal, Québec

Written by
Peter P. Harper

St. Lazarus Press
redroof.ca/st-lazarus-press

Copyright © 2023 The Church of St. John the Evangelist

All rights reserved.

No portion of this book may be reproduced in any form without written permission from the publisher or author, except as permitted by Canadian copyright law.

Foreword

This commentary on the liturgical year is a compilation with modifications of a series of notes prepared for the parish bulletin of the Church of St. John the Evangelist, Montreal, in 1988 and 1989. It is meant to give a historical perspective on the church year as it is celebrated in our parish, according to the traditional calendar of the Anglican Church of Canada. The parish is an Anglo-Catholic congregation that follows the Tractarian and Ritualistic traditions of the Church of England inspired by the Oxford Movement. Our liturgy is based on the 1959 Canadian *Book of Common Prayer*. The antiphons at high mass are taken from the Sarum Missal, the use of Salisbury Cathedral in the fifteenth century, a fine example of the Anglo-Norman Rite.

— Peter P. Harper

Contents

Introduction   1

Advent   3
   First Sunday in Advent 4
   Second Sunday in Advent 4
   Conception of the Blessed Virgin Mary 5
   Third Sunday in Advent 6
   Fourth Sunday in Advent 8

Nativity of Our Lord   9
   Christmas 12
   St. Stephen's Day 15
   St. John's Day 15
   Holy Innocents' Day 15
   Sunday within the Octave of Christmas 16
   Octave Day of Christmas 16

Epiphany of Our Lord   19
   Manifestation of Christ to the Gentiles 19
   Sunday within the Octave of Epiphany 22
   Sundays after Epiphany 23
   St. Peter's Chair 24
   St. Paul's Day 24
   Charles Stuart, King & Martyr 25

Presentation of Christ in the Temple 26
Sunday next before Septuagesima 28

Shrovetide   29
Septuagesima 30
Sexagesima 31
Quinquagesima 31

Lent   33
Ash Wednesday 34
First Sunday in Lent 36
Second Sunday in Lent 37
Third Sunday in Lent 38
Fourth Sunday in Lent 38
Fifth Sunday in Lent 40

Holy Week   43
Palm Sunday 43
Maundy Thursday 45
Good Friday 48
Tenebrae 52
Holy Saturday 53

Eastertide   57
Easter Day 57
Octave Day of Easter 60
Annunciation of the Blessed Virgin Mary 60
Rogation Sunday 62
Ascension Day 63
Sunday after Ascension Day 64
Whitsunday 64
Summer Ember Days 65

Trinitytide   67
Trinity Sunday 68
Feast of Corpus Christi 68
First Sunday after Trinity 70
Trinity 3 & 5 70
Nativity of St. John the Baptist 70

St. Peter & St. Paul	72
Visitation of the Blessed Virgin to Elizabeth	73
Lammas Day	74
Transfiguration of Our Lord	75
Most Sweet Name of Jesus	75
Falling Asleep of the Blessed Virgin Mary	76
Nativity of the Blessed Virgin Mary	78
Holy Cross Day	78
Autumn Ember Days	79
Trinity 18	80
St. Michael & All Angels	80
Dedication Festival	82
Thanksgiving	83
St. Simon the Zealot & St. Jude, Apostles	83
All Saints' Day	84
All Souls' Day	85
Feast of Christ the King	87

Bibliography   89

Introduction

The early church celebrated only Easter and perhaps also Pentecost, but soon hallowed all Sundays as feasts of the Resurrection.

The church year as we know it began to develop when the Church emerged from the period of persecutions in the early fourth century. It became customary for Christians in Jerusalem to visit the sites of the mysteries of Our Lord's life and death at various periods of the year for memorial services. The custom was copied in Rome, where the different basilicas and churches symbolically represented the various sites in the Holy Land and became stations for the feasts associated with these sites. From Rome, the practice spread to all Western churches.

The liturgical year developed around two major feasts:

(1) The *Easter (Atonement)* Cycle, based on a lunar calendar, centres around the variable date of Easter. It starts at Septuagesima and ends in Trinitytide.

(2) The *Christmas (Incarnation)* Cycle, oriented to a solar calendar, is based on the fixed date of Christmas. It begins with Advent and ends with Candlemas.

Both cycles make up the *Temporal*, *i.e.* the cycle of feasts reenacting the History of Salvation.

Superimposed upon this is the *Sanctoral*, which developed in a parallel manner and recalls the lives and witness of the saints. This seems to have grown primarily around the cult of martyrs during and after the persecutions.

There is, in a way, a conflict between the Temporal and the Sanctoral and, in the late Middle Ages, the Sanctoral almost dominated the Church Year. Our Reformers opted for a renewal of the Temporal and almost eliminated the Sanctoral from our Prayer Book. Some Reformed churches went so far as to eliminate the Temporal as well, retaining only the primitive church practice of hallowing Sundays or Sabbaths.

Advent

The *Advent* season, or *Winter-Lent*, has two parallel origins: one has a penitential character and comes from fifth-century Spain and Gaul where it was customary to fast three times a week from November 11 to Christmas during St. Martin's Lent. The other is from Rome and was a joyful preparation for Christmas which lasted four to five weeks and entailed no fasting except during Ember Days. The Oriental churches similarly observe St. Philip's Lent which begins on November 15.

Our present season dates from the thirteenth century and contains elements of both the penitential preparation for the end of the world and the joyful preparation for the commemoration of Christ's Nativity. This ambiguity is reflected in the liturgy where the vestments are purple and the *Gloria in excelsis* not sung (penitential), but the *Alleluia* is retained (joyful). The season can also be divided in two: a penitential period till December 17, and a joyful preparation in the last week.

The Advent wreath is of Lutheran origin and is part of German domestic practices. It is traditionally lit by a person named John or Joan, thus recalling John the Baptist who announced the coming of Jesus, the Light of the World.

First Sunday in Advent

The mass for the first Sunday is from the Sarum Missal, except for the collect which was composed in 1549 for the First Prayer Book. It is based on the Epistle and mentions the first and second comings of Christ.

The Gospel relating the entry of Christ into Jerusalem is the original reading for the day. It was replaced by that of the end of the world in the Roman Missal by Gregory the Great after a period of violent storms and cataclysms in Rome.

Second Sunday in Advent

Our service for this day follows the Sarum Missal, except for the collect which was written in 1549 by Archbishop Cranmer on the theme of the Epistle. Emphasis is placed on the image of Jerusalem and the coming of her Redeemer.

The Roman Church celebrates this feast at the Constantinian Basilica of *Santa Croce in Gerusalemme*, its symbolic Jerusalem.

The first sentence of the Epistle explains the choice of this Sunday as "Bible Sunday." The reading of the Gospel relating the destruction of Jerusalem follows ancient practice, such as the Lectionary (*Comes*) of St. Jerome, rather than the Roman Missal.

Our custom of repeating the Collect for Advent 1 as a "memorial" or seasonal collect after the collect of the day is of Gallican origin and was introduced in our use at the Savoy Conference by Bishop Wren (1662 Book of Common Prayer).

Conception of the Blessed Virgin Mary

Conception of St. Anne, December 8

This feast originated in the East (8th c.) and spread to the Gothic Church of Spain and to southern Italy where it was adopted by the Normans. Through them it reached England where it became the "Norman Festival." It occurred nonetheless in some early prayer books, such as the Leofric Missal (Exeter, 1050) and was celebrated before the Norman Conquest by black monks (Benedictines) at Canterbury. Its observance was apparently extended to the whole English Church by Lanfranc of Canterbury "upon occasion of William the Conqueror's fleet being in a storm, and afterwards coming safe to shore."

The Feast of the "Immaculate" Conception seems to have arisen in England where Eadmer, a Canterbury monk, defended the doctrine in his *Tractatus de conceptione Sanctae Mariae* (1224), and from there it spread to the continent. The Council of Oxford in 1220 left people free to observe the feast or not. It was nevertheless in general use by the mid-fourteenth century.

The concept of the Immaculate Conception was much debated by scholastic theologians; it was opposed by such eminent schoolmen as St. Thomas Aquinas and St. Bernard of Clairvaux, but supported by others such as Duns Scotus. The feast was extended to the Western Church by Sixtus IV (1476) and made mandatory by St. Pius V (1568). The Immaculate Conception of the Blessed Virgin Mary was proclaimed an article of faith by Pius IX in 1854 (*Ineffabilis Deus*).

The grey friars (Franciscans) were instrumental in the spread of this devotion, especially their *Doctor Subtilis*, John Duns Scotus (d. 1308). Indeed, a branch of this Order, the Recollects, introduced the devotion to New France and in 1608 dedicated our country to our Lady under the invocation of the Immaculate Conception.

The feast is also connected with the shrine of Lourdes in southern France. It was stricken from our First Prayer Book (1549) as non-scriptural, but was retained as a black-letter day.

The Nativity of the Blessed Virgin Mary is celebrated nine months later on September 8 next. The feast was originally on December 9, the fifth day before the Ides of December in the Roman calendar, as September 8 is the fifth before of the Ides of September.

Third Sunday in Advent

Gaudete Sunday

This is a Sunday of joy in anticipation of the coming of our Saviour, as indicated by the pink vestments, which are used by analogy with Refreshment Sunday in Lent.

The readings at mass are taken from the Sarum Missal, which follows ancient usage, rather than from the Roman Missal. The collect is that written in 1662 by Bishop Cosin at the Restoration to replace the ancient Roman Collect which was considered "too meagre." It is one of the few Collects in our Prayer Book to be addressed to Our Lord instead of to God the Father.

The Ember Days are held in the third week of Advent. In our Prayer Book their special theme is peace in the world.

December 16 (17 in the Roman calendar) is referred to in our calendar as O *Sapientia*. This alludes to the ancient custom, dating at least from Charlemagne's time (c. 800), of singing with great solemnity (rich vestments, bell ringing, etc.) special antiphons at the *Magnificat* of Vespers on this day and the following days. All these Greater Antiphons start with an O, hence their name of *The O's*. They are the theme of our annual Lessons and Carols service. The number of seven such antiphons has been fixed since the late Middle Ages in the Roman Church, but in many places there were more, up to twelve. Our mediæval forebears had noticed that if the initials of the second words are placed in order—

(1) O *Sapientia*

(2) O *Adonai*

(3) O *Radix Jesse*

(4) O *Clavis David*

(5) O *Oriens*

(6) O *Rex gentium*

(7) O *Emmanuel*

—and read from right to left, one gets *ERO CRAS*, which means "I will be (here) tomorrow." In English practice, there were usually nine antiphons, an additional one on December 21 in honour of St. Thomas, O *Thomas Didyme*, and another on December 23 in honour of our Lady, O *Virgo Virginum*.

It was also customary in many places to celebrate votive masses (*Rorate* masses) in honour of our Lady on each of the nine days before Christmas in order to commemorate her expectation. As these masses were celebrated before sunrise, and the people assembled in the church by torch light, this practice came to be known as that of the "Golden Nights." The Expectation of Mary was also the theme of the ancient mass on the Wednesday of Ember week which used the *Rorate* introit as well. It must be recalled that December 18 was the ancient feast day of the Annunciation and to this day a feast of the Expectation of Mary, "Our Lady of Hope," is observed on this date in Spain. In Celtic languages, Christmas Eve is referred to as "Mary's Night."

Fourth Sunday in Advent

Our service is taken integrally from the Sarum Missal, with the ancient readings from the *Comes* of St. Jerome and including the original collect from the Gelasian Sacramentary. This is the only one left of a set of three collects for Advent Sundays which were called the *Excita* ("stir up") collects from their opening word. The antiphons differ from those in the Roman Missal which have a more Marian character ("Hail Mary...," "Behold a Virgin...").

Nativity of Our Lord

The liturgical and folk customs we observe at Christmastide have diverse origins.

The *crib* was represented in Rome by a special chapel in the Basilica of St. Mary Major as early as 430. However, the popularity of cribs dates from 1223 when St. Francis of Assisi set one up in Greccio with real people and animals.

The *Christmas candle* represents Christ. In England it was usually made of three intertwined candles and decorated according to Anglo-Saxon practice with holly (the "holy tree," symbol of immortality, of the burning bush, of the thorns and blood of the Passion).

The *Christmas tree* has many origins: in mediæval times, it was customary to enact on December 24, the feast day of Adam and Eve, a mystery play depicting Paradise, the Fall, and the promise of a Redeemer. A tree bearing apples always figured prominently in this celebration and was called the Tree of Paradise.

Our Christmas tree is perhaps also related to Ygdrasil, the world-ash tree of Nordic mythologies, the tree sacred to the god Woden; St. Boniface, the apostle of Germany in the eighth century, introduced in its stead the image of the fir tree symbolizing eternal life. The tree we know today originated in Alsace in 1521 (1605?), spread to Germany where it was adorned with lights (17th c.), and in the nineteenth century passed to England (Queen Charlotte in 1800 and Prince Albert at Windsor in 1841).

Window lights are a Celtic custom.

Mistletoe, the sacred plant of the Druids, is a symbol of peace and reconciliation, hence the habit of kissing under the mistletoe. It represents the victory of an evergreen over the death of winter, and its medicinal properties recall Christ, "the Healing of the Nations." Its Celtic pagan origin has kept it out of churches. Fir, balsam, and ivy branches are commonly used for decoration and they represent eternal life.

The *Yule Log (Clog)* is of pagan origin. It is a large log laid across the hearth on Christmas Eve and lit with a branch from the previous year's log. It was originally associated with sun worship. The French Christmas cake, *la bûche de Noël*, recalls this ancient custom.

The *exchange of gifts* at this time of year was a Roman custom during the Saturnalia; the gifts were usually simple, wax candles or clay dolls, at least in the early period. St. Nicholas, a kindly fourth-century bishop of Myra in Asia Minor, is the patron saint of children and was traditionally associated with the giving of gifts to children, but also with their punishment, if need be, though he usually delegated this to a helper such as Knecht Rupprecht. By the end of the nineteenth century, he had unfortunately evolved into our secular and commercial Santa Claus.

The *singing of Christmas carols* dates from at least the fourteenth century, and the practice was very popular in Tudor and Stuart times. It was forbidden during the Commonwealth and it underwent a strong revival in the Victorian era.

Christmas cards became popular in the 1840s with the introduction of penny postage.

The *serving of a boar's head* is an ancient English custom related to Norse mythology. A boar was sacrificed to Freyr, the god of peace and plenty as well as of the golden sunshine, who was honoured at Yuletide and who was depicted riding the golden-bristled boar Gullinbursti brandishing his sword against the Frost Giants.

Also associated with Christmas is the *Glastonbury Thorn*. This is a hawthorn which flowers in southern England at about the time of Old Christmas (December 25 old-style, as in the Julian calendar, our January 7). This plant arose from a sprout off the common hawthorn which appeared in mediæval times at Glastonbury, and in which Arthurian legend recognized the staff of Joseph of Arimathea which sprouted when he supposedly came to Britain in 63 (61) to spread Christianity. The original shrub was cut down by Roundheads in 1653, but slips were taken by the faithful and the variety survived. The fact that the thorn did not flower on Christmas Day new-style in 1752 was taken as evidence that the then newly-adopted Gregorian calendar should not be followed.

Christmas

December 25

The birth of Our Lord in the year 4 BC (and not in year 0, or rather 1, as would be expected, because of an error of Dyonisius Exiquus in 533 in computing the years of the reign of Augustus) was not celebrated before the fourth century. It was recalled in the East on January 6 and in the West on December 25, the solstice in the Julian calendar.

After the end of persecutions, the Roman date prevailed (Julius I in 350) and the feast replaced the pagan celebration of the birthday of the "unconquered sun" (*Sol Invictus*) in the cult of Mithras. This period of the year was rich in festivals, such as the Roman Saturnalia in December, a celebration of the "good old days," and the various feasts of light associated with the solstice such as the nordic Yule bonfires in honour of Woden and Thor. The Anglo-Saxons celebrated the beginning of the year on this date and held a festival called Modranect or "Mothers' Night," a fertility celebration dedicated to the Norns or earth goddesses.

The Christian festival centers on Christ, the "Sun of Justice" (MAL 4:2). The original collect spoke of "this holy night [shining] with the illumination of the true light." Christmas marked the beginning of the church year (before the existence of Advent) and of the civil year in the High Middle Ages. It was introduced into England by Augustine (c. 600). It was suppressed by the Puritans during the Commonwealth (1649-1660) as contrary to the usage of the early church and replaced by a general market-day with a fast. Its strong revival in the nineteenth century is largely due to Charles Dickens' novels.

The custom of celebrating three masses on this day was a papal privilege which was extended to the Franks when they adopted the Roman Missal (c. 800) and passed on eventually to the rest of the Western Church. The first mass at cock-crow was at the crib erected since the times of Sixtus III (430) in *Santa Maria Maggiore*; it is the Angels' Mass. The second mass, at daybreak, originally for St. Anastasia, whose feast day it also is, was celebrated by the Byzantine colony of Rome, but was soon replaced by a Christmas mass, said of the Shepherds. The third mass originally at St. Peter's Vatican is the Great Mass, that of the Divine Word.

The mass we sing at midnight is the cock-crow mass (*Missa in gallicantu*) from the Sarum Missal. The procession to the crib is an ancient custom of the church in Bethlehem. Our morning masses are the original third mass.

The collect of the day is that written for the second mass in our First Prayer Book (1549). The additional collect proposed in our Prayer Book is that for Christmas Eve in Sarum use.

The name *Christmas* comes from the ancient (12th c.) English name of the feast, Christ's Mass (*Cristmasse*). This is a beautiful custom repeated in *Candlemas* and *Michaelmas*. It alludes to the fact that the mass is the central celebration of any festival. The word *mass* is from *missio*, the dismissal of catechumens and penitents before the offertory and that of the faithful at the end of the eucharistic service (*Ite, missa est*). The name came to be applied to the service as a whole as early as the fourth century (St. Ambrose) in Latin, as it did in many languages, but not in all. In Gaelic it is called *An aifrionn*, "the offering." The term *the Masse* still appears in our First Prayer Book (1549). At the Reformation, it was taken as referring to an unreformed service in contrast to the new service called Holy Communion and efforts were made to show that the *-mas* suffix derived from the Anglo-Saxon *maesse* (feast) rather than the Latin *missa*. The Oxford Movement restored the ancient name.

It is customary on this day, following the wish of St. Francis of Assisi, to give extra rations to animals.

This day is also the anniversary of many historical events, such as the Baptism of Clovis, King of the Franks (496), and the Coronations of Charlemagne (800), William the Conqueror (1066), and Baudouin the Crusader King of Jerusalem (1100). It was the privilege of the Holy Roman Emperor to read the Gospel at midnight mass with his sword drawn, following the example of Charlemagne.

The three next days are dedicated, respectively, to St. Stephen, to St. John the Evangelist, and to the Holy Innocents (*Childermas*). The services contain the ancient propers from the Sarum Missal, with expanded collects and a new Epistle appointed for St. John's Day in 1549. Thus, the Feast of Christ is associated with those of his saints, first with Stephen as is proper for the first martyr of the Church, then with John, the disciple Jesus loved, and finally with the Innocents who were the first to suffer upon our Saviour's account. "Martyrdom, Love, and Innocence are first to be magnify'd, as wherein Christ is most honour'd" (L'Estrange, 1690).

The merrymaking at this time of year is a very old tradition. The Roman Saturnalia in December in honour of Saturn, the father of the gods, were periods of intense merriment, from which came the ancient customs of the *Festum fatuorum* (Feast of the Fools or Daft Days) when ordinary people under the leadership of a Lord of Misrule, an Abbot of Unreason or a Fools' Bishop could, for a time, be free of society's constraints.

Traditionally, St. Stephen's Day was a free-for-all day for deacons, as was St. John the Evangelist's for priests, and the Holy Innocents' for choirboys. This led to the election of boy-bishops and mock ceremonies and sermons in churches. Such celebrations disappeared only in Tudor times. The Feast of the Asses (*Festum asinorum*) was similar, though less rowdy.

St. Stephen's Day

December 26

It was customary to bless horses on St. Stephen's Day together with the water and salt used for their care; pastries were also made in the form of horseshoes. The day was once known as Wrenning Day, when wrens were stoned in remembrance of St. Stephen's martyrdom.

St. John's Day

December 27

On St. John's Day wine was blessed. Commonly called the *Love of St. John*, the blessed wine was drunk not only on the feast, but also on great occasions throughout the year, such as weddings, departures on a trip, and on the deathbed.

Holy Innocents' Day

December 28

It was an ancient (and barbarous) custom to whip children on Childermas "that the memory of Herod's murder of the Innocents might stick the closer." An earlier feast for children on this day was transferred to December 6, St. Nicholas' Day, in the fifteenth century. Purple or even black vestments were used to signify the grief of the bereaved mothers, though now the use of white or red vestments prevails; the *Gloria in excelsis* and the *Alleluia* are omitted except on a Sunday. The day was considered ill-omened.

Sunday within the Octave of Christmas

Before the eighth century, Christmas had no Octave, so this Sunday was known as the First Sunday after Christmas. It originally celebrated the Presentation in the Temple. In the new Roman calendar, this is the feast of the Holy Family.

Octave Day of Christmas

Circumcision of Christ, New Year's Day, January 1

Since this feast falls on the Octave Day of Christmas, we use the collect and most of the propers of Christmas Day.

From the East came the custom of commemorating the Circumcision of Our Lord on this day, eight days after the Nativity; it spread to the West mainly through the Gallican and Gothic Churches (6th c.). Our second collect, from our First Prayer Book of 1549 but inspired by that in the Gregorian Sacramentary, recalls this event. Some English mediæval churches celebrated the Feast of the Most Sweet Name of Jesus (now on August 7) on this day, a practice reinstated in our alternative calendar (Book of Alternative Services 1985, The Naming of Jesus).

In Rome, there was a second mass in praise of our Lady. This is the oldest festival in her honour. The Eastern Church has a similar feast on December 26, the Synaxis of the All-Holy Mother of God. Indeed, in the present Roman Calendar (1969), the Octave Day of Christmas is the feast of St. Mary, Mother of God. This title of *Theotokos* ("God-bearer," Council of Ephesus, 431) was originally given in reaction to the Nestorians, who asserted that the human person of Jesus was united to but distinct from the Divine Word, thereby denying Mary's motherhood of God. No trace of this memorial has survived in our use.

Finally, in 1752, when England adopted the Gregorian calendar, January 1 again became the beginning of the civil year and this is recalled in our third collect, adapted from the Deposited Book (1928) of the Church of England. Scotland had adopted January 1 as New Year's Day in 1600 and this became a period of rejoicing particularly on the eve, known as Hogmanay.

In the early church, this was a fast-day (St. Augustine), because being the Kalends of January and in the late Roman Empire the first day of the year, it was a day of pagan revelling of such magnitude that St. Chrysostom speaks of the "Devil's Festival." A special mass "against idols" (*De idolis prohibendis*) used to be said.

It was a mediæval custom for fathers to bless their children and family on this day; the practice has survived in some places and was widespread in French Canada where it is still followed in many families. The Watch Night which consists in spending the last hour of the year in collective prayer arose in St. George's Methodist Church in Philadelphia and is still observed in many congregations.

Epiphany of Our Lord

Manifestation of Christ to the Gentiles

January 6

This, the Twelfth Day of Christmas, is the most ancient of the festivals which mark Christmastide. It originated in Egypt in the third century where a pagan festival was kept on this date in honour of the rising sun god.

It gained prominence in the fourth century as a proclamation of the Incarnation against the Arian heresy which denied Jesus' divine nature. The Gnostics (Basilidians) held this feast in great esteem and they stressed the Baptism of Christ because they believed that the Incarnation had occurred at that precise moment. By the mid-fourth century, the feast was celebrated in the West, and the Emperor Julian, later to be the Apostate, is known to have attended it in 361 in Vienne, in southern Gaul.

Its significance is that it commemorates the manifestation, or *epiphany*, of the Incarnate God. This has taken on multiple aspects, hence its name of "Day of the Epiphanies" (St. Jerome). In the early Jerusalem church it was the Nativity which was celebrated together with the revelation to the shepherds and the Magi. The Egyptian Church added the commemoration of Christ's Baptism and of "the first miracle that he wrought, in Cana of Galilee." Today in the Eastern Church only the Baptism is remembered in what is called the Feast of Holy Lights (the baptismal illumination of Christians). It is a special day for baptisms. The Monophysite Church of Armenia which has never accepted Christmas still celebrates the Nativity on this date.

In the Western Church, the three aspects are intermingled as witnessed by the antiphon of the *Magnificat*: "This day a star led the wise men to the manger, this day water was turned into wine at the marriage feast, this day Christ chose to be baptized by John...," but the main stress is on the manifestation to the Gentiles, hence its name of Three Kings' Day or The Stars (*Stellae*, in the eighth-century Celtic Stowe Missal). To this the Gothic Church added the manifestation of the multiplication of loaves. Since 1955 in the Roman Church, the Baptism of Christ is especially commemorated on the Octave Day, a practice followed by our 1959 Prayer Book. The Cana miracle is remembered on the Second Sunday after Epiphany. As well, the Baptism is recalled today at Mattins and the Cana Wedding at Evensong. The flight to Egypt is traditionally remembered on the vigil.

The Magi represent the Gentiles, and Tradition has given them names and origins: Gaspar (or Caspar), "king" of Tarsus; Melchior of Arabia; and Balthazar of Sheba. Other names are also available: Appelius, Amerus, and Damascus; Magalath, Galgaleth, and Sarasin; Ator, Sator, and Peratoras. Their respective gifts (from which their number was deduced) of myrrh, gold, and frankincense symbolize the attributes of the Saviour Child: humanity, kingship, and divinity.

Our service follows ancient practice, except the Epistle which was changed in 1549. The original Epistle is now part of the first lesson at Evensong.

As Easter is the next major festival in the church year and its date was for centuries a subject of much dispute, it was customary on this day for the Patriarch of Alexandria in Egypt to have a deacon proclaim after the Gospel (using the tone of the *Exsultet*) the date of Easter and other moveable feast days for the current year in a solemn declaration (*Epistola festalis*, Festal Letter); this custom was subsequently adopted by local bishops. Alexandria was given this honour at the Council of Nicaea (325) because of its reputation as a centre for astronomical study. From this arose the practice for bishops to deliver a pastoral letter on this day (later transferred to Lent).

It is also an ancient custom for bishops to bless water on the eve of Epiphany in a solemn ceremony; the water is then used to asperse the faithful as a memorial of their own baptism and to bless their dwellings. In the East, rivers such as the Nile, the Jordan, and in former times the Neva are blessed with great solemnity as a preparation for the baptisms. Before the Reformation, plays on the "Mystery of the Star" were performed in church and later on the church steps. These were the ancestors of the Epiphany masques and plays of the following centuries, the most famous of which is Shakespeare's *Twelfth Night*.

Since at least the fourteenth century, it has been the custom on the eve to bake a Twelfth-Night Cake containing a bean; the person receiving the bean becomes the "Bean King," the leader of the festivities. A piece is always kept for the poor (representing Jesus and Mary). Square mince-pies were also made, their shape recalling the manger and their filling the gifts of the Magi.

Like other Christian kings, the English sovereigns offer myrrh, gold, and incense in the Chapel Royal at St. James' Palace at the offertory of the mass. The twenty-five sovereigns of gold are eventually given to the poor, the incense used in church, and the myrrh given to a hospital. George III used to perform the ceremony accompanied by knights of the three great Orders; the rite is now usually performed by proxy by gentlemen-ushers.

Tomorrow is also Old Christmas Day, *i.e.* Christmas old-style (in the Julian calendar followed in England until 1752).

Sunday within the Octave of Epiphany

This Sunday is the last to deal with the childhood of Our Lord and in a sense it closes the Nativity Cycle, the month of the Child Jesus. Starting on the Octave Day of Epiphany, the Church introduces us to the public ministry of Jesus, beginning with the Baptism.

The propers are from the Sarum Missal. The collect, from the Gregorian Sacramentary, is one of the most beautiful in our Prayer Book. It relates to the Gospel in that Christian life involves both right knowledge and right practice.

Until 1969, the Roman Church celebrated on this day a special feast in honour of the Holy Family. This devotion was very popular in Quebec and it was introduced here in the early days of the colony by Bishop Laval and St. Marguerite Bourgeoys; all homes traditionally displayed a prominent picture of the Holy Family in the kitchen. The feast was celebrated here on Epiphany 2 long before it was introduced in the whole Roman Church in 1921 by Benedict XV. It was transferred to Epiphany 1 by Pius XI and it is now celebrated on the Sunday after Christmas or else on December 30.

In the Middle Ages, this was Plough Sunday, marking the end of the Christmas festivities and the return of men to work, most of them to plough or sow their fields. Ploughs were brought into church to be blessed. On the morrow, Plough Monday (or Plowlick Day), farmhands, their faces bleached and with cowhides on their backs, dragged a plough (called a fond, a fool, or a white plough) through the streets and begged money to buy votive candles, or plough-lights, to burn in church for a good harvest.

After the Reformation, the money was used for merry-making. The procession ended in festivities and a banquet presided over by a fool and a queen called a "Bessy" (often a man disguised as a woman). The Romans also held a ploughman's festival at this period, the *Compitalia*. January 7 marked the return of women to their work; this was called Rock Day, or humorously St. Distaff's Day, the rock or distaff being the stick used to hold the flax while spinning.

Sundays after Epiphany

On the second Sunday we celebrate the first miracle of Jesus at Cana. This introduction to the public life of Our Lord continues on the following Sundays.

The first five Sunday services are from the Sarum Missal where they were appointed for Sundays after the Octave of Epiphany. In our First Prayer Book (1549), the offices were brought forward one week. There was then a service missing for an eventual sixth Sunday and it was customary to repeat, when needed, the service for the fifth Sunday. At the Restoration (1662), a new service was written for this last Sunday by Bishop Cosin of Durham. The collect he provided is held to be the most beautiful of the "modern kind."

When Easter is early, we use only some of the post-Epiphany services. However, there are then more Sundays after Trinity and, instead of the missing services (Trinity 25 and 26), we use those of Epiphany 5 and 6, the Wandering Sundays, at the end of Trinitytide, where they are particularly appropriate.

Our service for the second Sunday uses the ancient Roman propers. The collect composed in the sixth century was selected for this day by the English monk Alcuin (8th c.); its original petition for peace in our time refers to the troubled times of the barbarian invasions.

St. Peter's Chair

January 18

January 18 was in the Roman Church the Feast of St. Peter's Chair, which recalled the bishopric of Peter in that city. A similar and much older festival of Gallican origin (6th c.) is still celebrated on February 22, at one time called St. Peter's Chair at Antioch, but now a general recollection of the ministry of Peter. The feast was instituted by Pope Pius IV in 1558 during the Council of Trent as a Counter-Reformation measure against those Reformers who denied Peter's presence at Rome and as a celebration of the primacy of the Roman See over the Universal Church.

Between this feast and that of St. Paul in the following week, the Conversion of St. Paul, January 25, it is customary in most Christian churches to celebrate the Church Unity Octave (now Christian Unity Week), a practice started by two Anglican priests, Fr. Wattson of New York and Fr. Spencer Jones of London in 1908, and popularized in the Roman Church by Fr. Couturier of Lyon in 1933, though it was commended by St. Pius X as early as 1909. The practice ultimately goes back to 1896 when Leo XIII asked Roman Catholics to pray for unity each year between Ascension Day and Pentecost. This is a period particularly designated for ecumenical encounters and for prayers for the Unity of Christians.

St. Paul's Day

January 25

The Conversion of St. Paul is the only feast of this apostle retained in our reformed calendar. It is of Gallican origin (6th c.) and was celebrated in Rome only from the tenth century.

The commemoration of St. Paul's Conversion rather than of his martyrdom probably reflects the capital significance of this event in the life and evolution of the early church. We have retained the original service, even the collect from the late Gregorian Sacramentary, which is exceptional for a saint's day.

In 1959, we restored a second feast in honour of St. Paul's death on June 29 together with that of St. Peter.

Charles Stuart, King & Martyr

January 30

On January 30, we commemorate the martyrdom of King Charles I, who was beheaded on order of the Rump Parliament in 1649 during the Great Rebellion.

This was originally a penitential service with fasting in reparation for the unlawful killing of an anointed king and the usurpation of royal prerogatives. The service was issued in 1662 at the Restoration and it contained "adulatory reverence for the sovereign and some bitter hatred of political enemies;" it was removed from the Prayer Book by Royal Warrant in 1859 as too political, and perhaps illegal. Our calendar nevertheless retains the commemoration of the event and it is customary in our parish to say the Mass of a Martyr on this day, while we recall the life, faith, and witness of Charles Stuart, a devout and saintly Christian. St. John's also possesses a relic of the Royal Martyr: a piece of his baptismal cloth, venerated at mass on this day.

Accompanied by his chaplain, Bishop William Juxon, the king mounted the scaffold and addressed the crowd. His last words were: "I go from a corruptible to an uncorruptible crown where no disturbance can be—no disturbance in the world."

Presentation of Christ in the Temple

Candlemas, February 2

This feast originated in the Orient in the fourth century and was held at the time on February 14, 40 days after the Epiphany, the commemoration of Christ's birth. It was moved to its present date when Christmas became widely accepted.

It seems to have spread under the Emperor Justinian as a thanksgiving festival following a plague (542). The feast was also known as the Meeting of Jesus with Simeon, the Day of Holy Simeon, and the Feast of Lights. It closes the Christmas cycle of our liturgical year, ending the *Quadragesima* (40 days) of the Epiphany (now Christmas).

By the year 700, under Pope Sergius I, the Roman Church celebrated on this day the Feast of the Purification of St. Mary the Virgin and held a solemn procession with tapers from the Church of St. Adrian in the Forum to St. Mary Major, a practice then common to all major festivals of our Lady. There was an ancient procession with lights during the *Lupercalia* in honour of Ceres (Februs) in ancient Rome on February 14–15, but there appears to be little or no connection between the two ceremonies, although some claim that the penitential character of the procession (purple vestments used to be worn) is in reparation for pagan excesses.

It has been a custom since the eighth century in Gaul to bless the year's supply of candles on this day. Candles usually of beeswax have been used in churches since the fourth century; two candles on the Altar have long been customary for mass in the Anglican Church and six (or seven) have been customary in the Roman Church for High Mass. They are used in a variety of other ceremonies. The symbolism of the lights refers to Simeon's canticle "A light to lighten the Gentiles," as well as to Christ "the Light of the world." The people customarily received a blessed candle from the priest on this day and held it during the procession, the reading of the Gospel and the canon. This explains the popular name of *Candlemas*. The blessed candle was brought home and lit on special occasions such as visitation, communion of the sick, or the deathbed agony of a loved one.

The service we sing on this day is the ancient mass from the Sarum Missal.

The purification of a woman after childbirth was a Jewish custom and consisted in offering a lamb or a pair of doves in a special sacrifice; Mary, being poor, offered doves.

Childbirth was considered to impart ceremonial uncleanness, probably by reference to original sin and the curse of our first parents ("Behold, I was brought forth in wickedness, and in sin hath my mother conceived me" (Ps 51:5)). As well, a first-born male child was considered to belong to God in a special way and reserved for the service of the Temple; he was usually bought back by an offering of money. While Jesus was offered at the Temple, there is no mention in the Gospel of the offering of money, though it is likely to have occurred. From this evolved our service for the Churching of Women. The old idea of uncleanness has disappeared, and the emphasis is now on thanksgiving for a safe delivery and the gift of a child; a gift to the church is still offered.

The baptismal or Chrisom robe of the child was often part of the offering, unless the child died within the month, in which case the "Chrisom child" would have been buried with it. Until the seventeenth century the woman wore a white veil.

It was customary in homes to light a candle in the evening, to make punch, and to let the children stay up till the candle had burned out. Christmas plants were burned on this day and the ashes spread over fields in hope of a good harvest. Graveyards were visited and prayers offered for the departed.

Candles were also blessed on the morrow, the Feast of St. Blasius; two of these were tied into a cross and held on each side of each person's neck while a benediction was said as a protection against sore throats. St. Blasius (d. 316) is said by legend to have saved a child choking on a fishbone and to have had his throat cut during his martyrdom. The custom still prevails in some Roman and Anglican churches.

Sunday next before Septuagesima

The next Sunday is Septuagesima and from that day the *Alleluia* will no longer be heard in the liturgy until the Great Vigil of Easter.

The *Alleluia* is last used at Vespers on the eve of Septuagesima when the service ends with the verse: ℣ *Benedicamus Domino, Alleluia, Alleluia.* ℟ *Deo gratias, Alleluia, Alleluia.* It was customary in the mediæval Church during these Vespers to give a solemn farewell, or funeral, to the *Alleluia* (*Depositio Alleluiae*). This involved a variety of ceremonies with the participation of children and special hymns were sung, one of which (# 63 in our Hymnal[1]) we sing on this day, our last solemn service before Septuagesima. Sometimes, a chorister representing the *Alleluia* was symbolically chased out of the church with a whip.

---

[1] "Alleluya, song of sweetness", The English Hymnal (1906)

Shrovetide

We start in this season the Paschal Cycle of the Church Year. As this is based on a lunar calendar, its dates vary from year to year. The next seventeen days form a short Pre-Lent period.

The habit of thus anticipating the Lenten season originated in Rome at the time of the barbarian invasions (mentioned as early as 465 by St. Maxim of Torino) and, during the bishopric of St. Gregory the Great (c. 600), special penitential masses were said. Our present services date also from those troubled times, probably after the invasion of the Lombards in 568, and indeed, its texts form the darkest and gloomiest selection of our liturgy, save only that of Good Friday. The major shrines of Rome were visited in pilgrimage as a plea for peace.

There is traditionally no *Gloria*, but a sober decoration of the altar is still allowed. This part of the church year has disappeared from both the new Roman Missal (1970) and our Book of Alternative Services (1985).

Septuagesima

This day had no special name at first, hence its ancient epithet of Lost Sunday. However, the name *Septuagesima* (from "seventieth day") came to be applied by reference to its position as third Sunday before *Quadragesima* (from "fortieth day") Sunday, anciently the first day of Lent, now our First Sunday in Lent. The reckoning is approximate, as this day is only the sixty-fourth day before Easter.

The Roman station on Septuagesima is at St. Lawrence Without, the least of the four Major Basilicas.

The choices of readings for the Epistle and the Gospel are interesting in that the former stresses that it is never too late to be damned and the latter that it is never too late to be saved.

This is traditionally for monks the beginning of the Great Lenten Fast (*Caput ieiunii*), and in some Oriental Churches, the fast starts the next day for all, in which case it is held four days a week, Wednesdays, Saturdays, and Sundays being excluded, except during Holy Week.

In the early Roman Empire, the civic new year started on the Kalends of March (the first) and this coincided roughly with this part of the church year. This is perhaps reflected in the universal custom in the Church of beginning the serial reading of the Bible on this day, and that is why we return to the first chapters of Genesis as Old Testament lessons at Mattins and Evensong.

In the Middle Ages, when the lessons were read only at Mattins and therefore extended over a longer period, Septuagesima week was known as Adam's Week, and the next two as Noah's Week and Abraham's Week.

Sexagesima

This is the second Sunday of the Pre-Lent season and its name, *Sexagesima* (from "sixtieth day," actually the fifty-seventh), parallels those of the other Sundays. This is also the beginning of the eight-week Lent in many Eastern Churches in which fasting is not observed on Saturdays or Sundays.

The Roman Christians continued their penitential pilgrimages for peace on this day, and they assembled at the Basilica of St. Paul Without. This was alluded to in the ancient formulation of the collect which read "by the protection of the Teacher of the Gentiles," replaced by Cranmer with by "thy power." The propers again this week reflect the hard times of the period, that is the barbarian invasions of the sixth and seventh centuries.

Quinguagesima

This is the third Sunday of Pre-Lent and called *Quinquagesima* since it is the fiftieth day before Easter. The penitential pilgrimages for peace of the early Roman Church continued on this day and the people assembled at St. Peter's Vatican Hill, the second in dignity of the Major Basilicas.

The service dates from the seventh century, but the collect has been replaced by a new one written by Cranmer on the theme of the Epistle (love); the old collect referred to the mediæval custom of going to confession (*shriving*, from the Old English *scrifan*), a practice which, when treated as obligatory, our Reformers did not approve of. The collect read in part: "having loosed us from the bonds of our sins, keep us from all adversity." The next day was traditionally for the clergy the beginning of the Great Fast.

Quinquagesima is also known as Carnival Sunday (*Dominica carnevala*) in reference to the festivities which mark the last days before Lent. The next day is Collop ("slice," "morsel") Monday, when any leftover meat was eaten before Lent or else cut into strips and dried for keeping. Tuesday is a day of revelling and is known variously as Shrove (Confession) Tuesday, Pancake Tuesday, Fat Tuesday (*Mardi gras*), and Doughnut Tuesday. The custom of eating pancakes, after the toll of the Pancake Bell (Great Bell or Confession Bell), is related to the fact that eggs and fat were forbidden during Lent and this was the last chance to enjoy this food. In France, "French" toast was also eaten (*Jour de pain perdu*). In French, the three "fat" days before Lent were sometimes mockingly referred to as the feasts of Ss. Goulard, Pansard and Dégobillard (respectively "glutton," "fat-bellied," and "retcher").

The whole three-day period had either a penitential character (Shrovetide for priests and the people who had been shriven), or a joyful one (Carnival or Good-tide for the others). The term *Carnival* comes from *caro, carnis* (meat) and *levarium* ("lifting," "taking away") and refers to the coming abstinence.

Lent

The name *Lent* comes from the Old English *lencthen* and refers to the season of lengthening days or spring.

The custom of fasting before Easter started with a forty-hour fast (Our Lord's stay in the grave), which gradually extended to Holy Week, then to six weeks by the fourth century. Lent still starts on the next Monday in the Ambrosian rite of Milan. This was the tenth part or *tithe* of the year. The forty days recall the fasts of Moses, Elijah, and Jesus, as well as the forty days of the Flood, and the forty years in the wilderness.

Mourning clothes were worn during Lent, a practice followed by Queen Elizabeth I. Similarly, white or purple Lenten arrays were hung in churches, hiding crosses, statues, and sometimes the whole sanctuary from the view of the people (nowadays, usually restricted to the reredos, or, in Roman use, to crosses and statues, but only from Passion Sunday). Social activities (balls, concerts, etc.) and hunting were forbidden. Wars were interrupted (Truce of God). Law courts were closed. Sexual intercourse was proscribed and no marriage could be performed.

In Eastern Churches, mass is offered only on Sundays and Saturdays; on other days Masses of the Presanctified (without consecration) are said using the elements consecrated on the previous Sunday.

In early times, Lent was very strict; meat, eggs, cheese, butter, fats, and wine were prohibited for the duration, even on Sundays, but some foods were favoured, for instance, "Lenten fig(ge)s." Only one meal a day was allowed, in the evening after Vespers. This led eventually by the fifteenth century to the anticipation of Vespers to midday on weekdays, starting on the first Monday in Lent. Monks who worked outdoors were later permitted a little wine in the evening as a collation (*collatio*, or "conference," because the wine was drunk during the evening reading of the *Conferences* of Cassian and other Holy Fathers held before Compline), later accompanied by a piece of bread, "lest the drink ruin the stomach."

By the nineteenth century, the Roman Church allowed breakfast and the use of milk products in return for almsgiving. Fasting is commended in the Fourth Homily "to chastise the flesh that it be not too wanton, but tamed and brought into subjection to the spirit... that the spirit may be more fervent and earnest in prayer... that our fast be a testimony and witness with us before God, of our humble submission to his high majesty."

Ash Wednesday

Ash Wednesday, known also as Head of the Fast, marks the beginning of Lent since the pontificate of Gregory II (c. 720).

The ashes were part of a ritual used for public penitents. In the early church, public sinners were excluded from the Eucharist and had to be reconciled after a public penance of forty days (quarantine) or even of years (hence the habit of counting indulgences in years and quarantines). The penance was often long, and four-year sentences were common.

The first year, the penitents, or *flentes* ("mourners"), wept before the door of the church; the second year, *audientes* ("hearers") were allowed to listen to the readings (first part of the mass); the third year, *substrati* ("kneelers") could kneel among the faithful; and the fourth year, *consistentes* ("co-standers") could stand in the congregation. All were excluded from the sacraments and special collects "over the bowed heads" were said for them.

The sinners came to church on Ash Wednesday, barefoot and dressed in sackcloth; after the penitential psalms had been recited, the bishop laid hands on them, and sprinkled them with holy water. They had ashes put on their head ("Remember that thou art dust..."), and were expelled from the church by the bishop repeating over them the curse of Adam and Eve ("In the sweat of thy brow shalt thou eat thy bread..." (GEN 3:19)).

This curse later became the Greater Excommunication which our Reformers made into a "Commination (Threatening) or Denouncing of God's Anger and Judgements against Sinners" (our penitential service). By the eleventh century (Council of Benevento, 1091), it had become the custom for all to go and receive the ashes as a sign of penitence and public sinners were no longer singled out. The Council of Trent in the sixteenth century tried but failed to revive the ancient practice.

The service for Ash Wednesday is the mass from the Sarum Missal for which Cranmer composed a new collect, inspired by the old collect for the blessing of ashes.

Special pastries (flour, salt, water but no eggs) were cooked on this day symbolizing the crossed arms of a praying person, and these *bracellae* are the ancestors of our pretzels.

First Sunday in Lent

Shrove Sunday

As the Fast was not observed on Sundays, though abstinence continued, Sundays are said to be "in" Lent rather than "of" Lent.

This First Sunday was known as *Invocabit* Sunday from the opening word of the *officium* (introit). The collect was rewritten in 1549 by Cranmer; it is the first to refer to the Great Fast, probably because the next day marked the beginning of Lent in early times. The original version in the First Prayer Book mentioned "our flesh being subdued to the spirit" (*i.e.* our spirit) rather than "to the Spirit" (the Holy Ghost). The old Sarum collect implied that fasting and good works could be means of acquiring merit and it did not meet with the approval of our Reformers (Article XII); it read "grant to thy family that what it strives to obtain from thee by fasting, it may follow up by good works."

Psalm 51, "Whoso dwelleth," is used for all the antiphons except the Communion and it is appropriate both in content and from its use in the Gospel narrative of Our Lord's temptations.

The Church at Rome congregated as it did in the three preceding Sundays in a Major Basilica, on this day in the foremost, St. John Lateran (anciently the Holy Saviour), the cathedral of Rome, and the "mother and head of all churches."

In France, youths came to church on this day carrying torches in order to amend their excesses in the carnival of the preceding week; it was the *Dimanche des brandons* (Sunday of Torches).

The Lenten Ember Days occur this week and special prayers are offered in our use for "missionary work in our own country." These are the most recent of the four series of Ember Days. They were held at first during the first week of

March and were transferred to the first week of Lent in the eleventh century in order not to multiply days of penitence.

It was customary in the ancient Roman Church for the Pope to go in procession to say mass each day of Lent in a different *station church* of the city, a practice revived by Pope John XXIII. There was a special service written for each day except for Thursdays (which were added only in the eighth century). These masses were still present in our pre-Reformation missals; they have not been retained in our Prayer Books, but many of the original readings have been restored in the Eucharist lectionary of the Book of Alternative Services. Many churches imitated the Roman use and held penitential processions, particularly on Wednesdays and Fridays.

Second Sunday in Lent

This day was known as *Reminiscere* Sunday from the first word of the *officium* (introit). It was originally a vacant Sunday because the Ember Vigil Service on Saturday, with its twelve lessons and successive ordinations, extended through the night. The propers were borrowed from other days at a later date.

The collect is an expansion of the original from the Gregorian Sacramentary. The readings are from the selection in the Sarum Missal. The Roman Church used the Gospel narrative of the Transfiguration on this day, having placed the story of the woman of Canaan on the preceding Thursday.

Third Sunday in Lent

Known as *Oculi* Sunday from its *officium* (introit), this was also called in the early Roman Church "Scrutiny Sunday," because candidates for baptism were examined on this day, a practice later transferred to Wednesday of the next week. The whole congregation was called upon to testify on the life and morals of the catechumens.

The collect is the original from the Gregorian Sacramentary, though expanded. The readings are the same as in the Roman and Sarum Missals. The reference to light in the Epistle alludes to an inscription in the Basilica of St. Lawrence, the station church.

Fourth Sunday in Lent

Refreshment Sunday

Called *Laetare* Sunday from its *officium* (introit), this day is also known as Refreshment Sunday, Mid-Lent Sunday, Mothering Sunday, Jerusalem Sunday, New Sunday, Rose Sunday, Alb Sunday, and Sunday of the Five Loaves.

On this Sunday, we temper the ascetism of Lent. On the previous Thursday, twenty of the forty days have passed. We pause a little before taking on the second half.

The service contains the ancient Gregorian collect which speaks of the "comfort of thy grace" and the Gospel relates the feeding of the multitude. Popes traditionally distributed bread to the poor in re-enactment of this event.

The Epistle refers to "Jerusalem which is the mother of us all," and it was a custom in many cities to visit the main or mother church of the area; thus, the Romans assemble in the Basilica of the Holy Cross (*S. Croce in Gerusalemme*), their symbolic Jerusalem (this is perhaps also related to the fact that Eastern churches celebrate Holy Cross Day on this Sunday). The reference to "mother" led to the English custom of visiting one's mother on this day. Special pastries called *Simnel* or Mothering cakes and violets were brought as gifts. There was a similar pagan festival at this time on the Ides of March, that of Hilaria, the Mother of the Gods, which was associated with family reunions. There may be no connection between the two feasts.

The Pope sometimes blesses a Golden Rose (an natural rose in earlier times, but since the eleventh century a gold ornament) on this day and anoints it with chrism and scents it with balsam and musk in remembrance of "the root of Jesse." The rose is sent to a sovereign, a dignitary, a church, or a city which is to be honoured. Henry VIII received one from three different popes. This custom is recalled in our use of rose-coloured vestments on this Sunday.

Wednesday next in the early Roman Church was the day of the Great Scrutiny when catechumens were given an important test as preparation for their baptism at the Easter Vigil. They were sealed (signed with the cross) by their sponsors, submitted to exorcisms and read the prophets (EZEK 31:23–8, Is. 1:16–19). Salt was put on their tongues. Their ears were symbolically unstopped with the *Ephphatha*. They were then initiated to some of the "secrets" of the Church (*Traditio symbolorum*): the four Gospels (the opening verses of each were read), the Symbols (the Apostles' Creed, and at a later date the Nicene Creed, read to them in Greek and Latin), and the Lord's Prayer (explained to them). After the Gospel of the Healing of the Blind Man, they left the church, but were especially remembered in the intercession. Part of this ceremony has survived in our baptismal rite, particularly that for "such as are of riper years," in the Creed and the supplication before baptism.

Fifth Sunday in Lent

Passion Sunday

The Epistle contains a clear reference to the Passion, hence the name given to this Sunday since the ninth century. Other names include Care (Suffering) Sunday and Black Sunday.

The service is ancient and has retained its original elements. In early times, the Gospel used to be that of the Resurrection of Lazarus, but the present selection is more appropriate to the day. The *Gloria Patri* doxology is no longer said till Easter, partly as a sign of mourning, but also because the service precedes the introduction of the doxology, and ancient practice still prevails on this day (as it does in requiem masses, which are also very ancient). Psalm 43, "Give sentence," used in the *officium* (introit), is therefore omitted in the priest's private preparatory prayers. Hence also the name *Judica* Sunday.

Since the third century, Passion Sunday has marked the beginning of the Passion Fortnight or Passiontide, a period of special devotion which was kept even before the institution of the forty-day Lent. In Roman use, crosses and images are veiled with purple until Good Friday (crosses) or Easter Vigil (images and statues). This is said to be related to the last sentence of the Roman Missal's appointed Gospel: "but Jesus hid himself..." (JOHN 8:59), but this doubtless is an afterthought; the 1959 revision of our Book of Common Prayer instead appoints a Gospel from Matthew: "Even as the Son of man came not to be ministered unto, but to minister, and to give his life a ransom for many" (MATT 20:20–28). In English use, crosses and statues are covered with white Lenten arrays throughout Lent. The liturgical colour in mediæval England for Passiontide was red, and contrasted with that of Lent which was white (unbleached linen). We generally adopt the Roman purple for the whole period, except on weekdays during Passiontide when red is used.

It is traditional in the north of England to eat parched beans fried in butter on this day; these are known as carlings, hence the name Carling or Carle Sunday.

Friday of this week is the Feast of our Lady of the Seven Sorrows (Dolors), recalling the suffering of our Lady during the Passion. It was instituted by a Synod in Cologne in 1423 and extended to the whole Roman Church by Benedict XIII in 1727. With this feast is associated the beautiful mediæval hymn *Stabat Mater* (# 115[2]) by the Franciscan Tertiary Jacopone da Todi (1228–1306). It is one of the great lyrical poems of its time and we commonly use it on this Sunday and during the Stations of the Cross.

---

[2] "At the Cross her station keeping", The English Hymnal (1906)

Holy Week

Palm Sunday

Sunday next before Easter

This day is known by various names, such as Second Passion Sunday, Flowering Sunday, Willow Sunday, Blossom Sunday, Sallow Sunday, Palm Easter, Fig Sunday, Yew Sunday, most of them referring to the Procession recalling the solemn entry of Our Lord into Jerusalem, but also as Alm Sunday ("Ye have the poor with you always" (MARK 14:7)) and Tradition Sunday (giving of the Creeds to catechumens). It marks the beginning of the Great Week or Holy Week, also known as Mute Week, Black Week, Ultimate Week, Penitential Week, and Indulgence Week.

The procession was first reenacted by the Church of Jerusalem as early as the third century. It started on the Mount of Olives, and the Patriarch riding an ass was escorted to the Church of the Resurrection or to Mount Sion by the people carrying palms and singing *Hosanna*. The blessing of the palms is a Gallican custom, probably from eighth-century Germany. In traditional use this blessing was very elaborate and formed a kind of dry mass (a mass without consecration) containing a collect, an Epistle, a Gospel, a preface, a *Sanctus* and five additional collects.

In England, willows, box, and yew were traditionally used, while olive and palm branches were customary in southern Europe. Flowers were also blessed. In mediæval England in Hereford use, after the blessing of the branches, the procession went to the chapel (or tent) without the city walls where the Reserved Sacrament had been conveyed privately. After adoration, the Sacrament was taken and carried in procession on a feretory by two priests. It was therefore a *Corps saint* procession in the Norman manner.

As the procession approached the city, children on the gate sang *Gloria, Laus* (# 621, # 622)[3], the traditional hymn by Theodulph of Orleans (d. 821). On entering the church, the Sacrament was held aloft transversely in the doorway and the procession passed under it. When it reached the Rood or Great Cross, the hymn *Ave Rex Noster* was sung (App. # 3).[4] The procession often ended with a visit to the graveyard.

The procession was abolished in the First Prayer Book (1549), but the custom persisted of decking the church with willow branches; children carried slips of willow and graves were strewn with flowers. The practice was revived in the nineteenth century, and the Gospel of the triumphal entrance of Christ was restored as the second lesson at Evensong in 1871.

The mass is of the Passion, with the ancient collect from the Gelasian Sacramentary, which is a marvelous statement on the Atonement. The Epistle speaks of the glory of the Christ and it is customary to kneel at "at the name of Jesus every knee should bow" (Phil 2:10). The Gospel narrates the Passion according to Matthew as prescribed in the *Comes* of

---

[3] "Glory and praise and dominion be thine, King Christ the Redeemer", "All glory, laud, and honour", The English Hymnal (1906)
[4] *Ibid.*

St. Jerome (390) and was solemnly sung by three deacons (a tenor being the narrator, a bass representing Christ, and an alto the others), a custom originating in northern Europe in the tenth century. When it was read that "the veil of the temple was rent in twain," the great Lenten veil (which in English custom hid the sanctuary from the people during Lent) was divided and drawn aside. The English liturgical colour for this day is red; the purple we use is of Roman origin.

Pax cakes were cooked on this day in England and given to persons with whom one wished to be reconciled, as a preparation for the Easter communion.

On Monday and Tuesday, the Passion according to Mark is read at mass in Anglican use. In early times, it was not read because it was thought to be a summary of Matthew's account (it is in fact more ancient) or else it was read on Saturday. In Sarum use, Mark's narrative was read on Tuesday, and Luke's on Wednesday. A new Epistle was appointed for Wednesday in 1549 (the continuation of that of Passion Sunday, to be followed up on Good Friday). The old Epistle is now on Monday and that of Monday has moved to Tuesday.

Wednesday is known as Spy Wednesday, recalling Judas' visit to the priests and his willingness to act as their agent. Spring cleaning was traditionally done on these days.

Maundy Thursday

The name *Maundy* comes from the Middle English *Maundee* which means "command" (*Mandatum*), from the words of Our Lord ("A new commandment I give unto you" (JOHN 13:34)). In Wales this is the Thursday of Blasphemy, recalling the mocking of Jesus at his trial.

There were traditionally three masses on this day. The first in the morning was that of the reconciliation of the penitents who had been excluded from the church since Ash Wednesday.

The penitents were prostrate at the door of the church while the Penitential Psalms (6, 32, 38, 51, 102, 130, and 143) and the Litany were sung. They were received by the bishop, and after a preface and more sung psalms (50, 55, 56), they were given absolution. They afterwards went home to wash, shave, and put on new clothes. Church doors were left open on this day to symbolize the Church's hearty reception of sinners. This was a day of reconciliation, and loving cups were drunk. Yet from 1364 to 1773 popes proclaimed a bull on this day listing the names of the newly excommunicate and the notorious heretics.

The practice of washing was also followed by monks since the time of St. Augustine and some even took baths ("not my feet only, but also my hands and my head" (JOHN 13:9)). This explains the name Shore Thursday when monks shaved their heads ("For in olde faders dayes men would make hem that day shere hemm and pollen her heedes and clippen her beards and so make hem honeste ageyn ester day," *Liber Festivalis*, 1483). The name Shore Thursday could also have originated from *shier* ("pain"). The catechumens were also washed in preparation for their baptism on Easter Vigil. They were asked to rehearse the Creed which they had learnt two weeks earlier (*Redditio symboli*).

The second mass, in late morning, is the Chrismal Mass in which the bishop, assisted by twelve priests, seven deacons and seven subdeacons, blesses the olive oil needed for the church services: during the canon, the oil for the anointing of the sick (also used for the blessing of church bells); after communion, the oil of catechumens for use at baptism, blessing of the font, ordination of priests, consecration of altars, and coronation of sovereigns; also the chrism, a mixture of oil and balm, used for blessing the font and for baptism, confirmation, consecration of bishops, consecration of churches, altars, sacred vessels, and bells. The use of oil in our church disappeared in the Second Prayer Book (1552), but was partly restored in our 1959 Book of Common Prayer and extended in the Book of Alternative Services.

The third mass in the evening (the only such occasion until recent times) recalls the Institution of the Blessed Sacrament, the Lord's Supper. The Celtic Church called this day the Birthday of the Chalice (Stowe Missal, 8th c.). This is a festal mass, yet it has no Creed (an ancient practice) and the peace is not given (perhaps because of Judas's kiss on this day). During the *Gloria*, bells are rung after which they are silent, as is the organ, until the *Gloria* on Easter Eve; the bells are usually replaced by a watchman's rattle or crotalus. We usually say the Mass of Corpus Christi instead of the Prayer Book service which recalls both the Sacrament (Epistle and second collect) and the Passion (Gospel and first collect).[5] The Epistle is Paul's account of the Institution, the oldest such narrative that the Church possesses.

During this mass, it is traditional for the celebrant to reenact Our Lord's washing of the feet of the apostles, by washing and kissing the feet of twelve persons (*Lavipedium*). Sometimes a thirteenth person represents Christ or, perhaps, an angel.

This was also done by various dignitaries. English sovereigns customarily washed the feet of as many poor persons as years in their reign or life; they then gave them gifts of clothing, food, and money. This is the Royal Maundy or Royal Maunds. Queen Elizabeth I did it every year and James II (r. 1685–1688) was the last king to observe the custom. The ceremony was later taken over in the king's name by the Archbishop of York until 1731. It has been continued, but without the washing, by the Lord High Almoner (the Clerk of the Almonry since 1883) who, girded with a long towel, distributed clothes and money to aged poor people at the

---

[5] Since the author's writing, it has become customary to read the Maundy Gospel (John 13:1-11) instead of St. Luke's Passion narrative appointed by the 1959 Book of Common Prayer. While the parish now uses the major and minor propers of Maundy Thursday (excepting the foregoing), the appointed second collect (sometimes said alone) and Epistle nevertheless derive directly from the Mass of Corpus Christi.

Chapel Royal in Whitehall. The custom is now performed at a different cathedral each year and the sovereign is often present (both King George V in 1932 and King Edward VIII in 1936 participated actively in the distribution).

The service has the form of Mattins until after the First Lesson (John 13:1–16), when a first distribution is made in lieu of clothing (£1/15/- to women, £2/5/- to men) during the First Anthem. During the Third Anthem, there is a second distribution of red purses in lieu of provisions in kind (£1 gold, plus £1/10/-) and then of white purses containing as many pence as the age of the sovereign. Two collects (for the sovereign and for the day) end the service. Since the time of Charles II, coins of obsolete denominations and with unmilled edges ("maundy money") are especially minted by the Royal Mint for the occasion.

The Sacrament is reserved after mass at the Altar of Repose where it is adored through the night by the faithful. In earlier times, only the priest communicated on Good Friday, so only one host was reserved. In England a supplementary host was consecrated to be put in the sepulchre on Good Friday. It is customary to visit the altars of repose in seven different churches, recalling the Romans' habit of visiting seven basilicas.

A shortened form of Vespers was then sung. As Psalm 22 is read, the main altar is stripped of its linen and ornaments, recalling the stripping of Our Lord. In mediæval times, stone altars were washed with wine and water.

Good Friday

The name *Good Friday* probably comes from *God's Friday*, or perhaps "good" means "holy." The day is also called the Day of Preparation (*Parasceve* in the Roman Missal), Day of Absolution, Char Friday, or Long Friday.

Mourning is prescribed on this day in the fourth-century *Apostolic Constitutions*. There is no mass, and in the Gothic Church of Spain churches were closed. In the Middle Ages, the sacrament was reserved for the communion of the sole celebrant and later only the consecrated bread was reserved, to be taken with unconsecrated wine. Happily, the practice of universal communion in both kinds has been restored.

The Communion service from the reserved elements is known as a Mass of the Presanctified (Elements) and is widespread in Eastern Churches on penitential days, particularly during Lent. Our Prayer Book does not forbid a full Communion service on this day, and this was the practice in the reigns of Elizabeth I and James I, but it is now customary to hold no more than an Ante-Communion service or else a Mass of the Presanctified. The use of black vestments today is a Roman custom. The English Church used red.

Our service in the 1980s began with the unveiling of the cross, which occurred after the Passion Gospel in mediæval uses. In the Roman Church, the priest takes off his vestment in remembrance of Emperor Heraclius who carried the relic of the True Cross back to Jerusalem after having taken off his royal vestments. The cross was unveiled gradually by the priest singing three times "Behold the wood of the Cross." It was then set on a cushion on the altar steps; the priest and all the clergy took off their shoes and, doing three double genuflections, came to kiss the cross. The practice was known as "creepynge of the crosse [which] signifyeth a humblynge of ourselfe to Christe before the Crosse, and the kissinge of it as a memorie of our redemption" (Henry VIII). The Reproaches, or *Improperia* (# 737[6]), of Mozarabic origin from Micah 6:3–4, with the Oriental *Trisagion* in Greek and Latin, were sung during this ceremony, as was the hymn *Vexilla Regis* (# 94[7]) composed by Venantius Fortunatus, Bishop of Poitiers, for the reception of a relic of the Holy Cross. Indeed in Jerusalem the

---

[6] "O my people, what have I done unto thee?", The English Hymnal (1906)
[7] "The royal banners forward go", *Ibid.*

relic was "adored" yearly on this day till its disappearance in 1187. The Roman people also came to the Basilica of the Holy Cross to venerate their relic and touch it with their foreheads. The unveiled cross was then deposited in a sepulchre on the north wall of the chancel (together with a Host consecrated on Thursday in Sarum use) and in some uses washed with wine and water. It is customary on this day to genuflect as one passes before an unveiled cross.

The collects follow. There are only three left in our Prayer Book from the original eight (Sarum) or nine (Rome), and the third is now omitted. The first is from the 1552 Prayer Book and was taken from Mattins in the 1549 Book and is the *oratio super populum* from Holy Wednesday (the day of the betrayal) in ancient use. The second for the clergy and people is the original third collect. The third is a summary of the original seventh, eighth, and ninth collects, and it used to list Jews, Turks (Muslims), Infidels, and Heretics. People knelt for the collects except (until 1955) for that for the Jews, so completely did prejudice triumph over the teaching of the day.[8] The other ancient collects were for the Church, the Pope, the Roman Emperor, the catechumens, and all human problems.

---

[8] Canon XIV of the Anglican Church of Canada, promulgated by General Synod in 1992, formally rescinded the third collect from the 1959 Prayer Book, requiring that it be "deleted from use and from further printings of the Book of Common Prayer." In 2023, a deprecated related prayer *For the Conversion of the Jews* (Occasional Prayer 4, p. 41) was also rescinded, replaced by the following prayer *For Reconciliation with the Jewish People* developed by the Prayer Book Society of Canada:

> O God, who didst choose Israel to be thine inheritance: have mercy upon us and forgive us for violence and wickedness against our brother Jacob; the arrogance of our hearts and minds hath deceived us, and shame hath covered our face. Take away all pride and prejudice in us, and grant that we, together with the people whom thou didst first make thine own, may attain to the fulness of redemption which thou hast promised; to the honour and glory of thy most holy Name. Amen.

The Epistle was chosen in 1549 and it is a continuation of that of Wednesday. It replaced two readings of the Old Testament (Hosea 6:1-6 and Exodus 12:1-11). The traditional Gospel of the day is the Passion according to St. John who witnessed the events. The narrative is begun at Mattins.

The "mass" is a communion with the canon and *Agnus Dei* omitted, but with most other parts retained.

In Roman and Sarum uses, the order of the service was different: it began with a prostration of the clergy on the floor of the chancel. Then followed two collects, two lessons with tracts, and the reading of the Passion. The eight or nine "catholic" collects were said, these being the original form of the intercession at the offertory. Veneration of the Cross and communion then followed.

In the early church of Jerusalem, the people assembled in the Garden of Gethsemane to read the treason narrative and returned to Jerusalem for the other services.

Other devotions for the day include the Passion Hours or *Tre Ore*, originally a meditation on the seven words of Christ from the sixth to the ninth hour (noon – 3 p.m.) instituted by Father Alfonso Mesia in Peru in 1687. The devotions of forty hours (Christ's lying in the grave) also originated on Good Friday. The Stations of the Cross are a devotion invented by the Crusaders and recall their visits to the settings of Christ's Passion, and their following our Saviour's steps along the *Via Dolorosa*. Oriental Churches have an additional service called the *Epitaphion* which is a symbolic burial of Christ, and in the evening a procession which is a sort of a funeral service.

English kings blessed cramp-rings on this day as a protection against falling-sickness. Hot cross buns were baked from flour usually reserved for the baking of Eucharistic bread.

Tenebrae

The Mattins and Lauds of the three last days of Holy Week, the *Triduum Sacrum*, were celebrated in a particular manner on the preceding evening, in the dark, hence the name *Tenebrae* ("darkness").

The service had the ancient simple form without later embellishments. The first part was Mattins proper, *i.e.* three nocturns consisting each of three psalms with antiphons and three lessons with responsories. The second part was Lauds made up of five psalms, the *Benedictus*, and the final antiphon "Christ became obedient unto death." The first set of lessons was from the Lamentations of Jeremiah, the second set from the Commentaries of St. Augustine on the Psalms, and the third from the Epistles of St. Paul.

The church was dark and a great triangular taper-hearse was set in the middle of the chancel bearing fifteen tapers (twenty in Sarum use) of yellow wax; six candles were also lit on the altar. One taper on the hearse was extinguished after each of the fourteen psalms. During the *Benedictus* the altar candles were also extinguished. The last taper was taken from the hearse and hidden behind the altar during the last antiphon; after a moment of silence, a noise was made (this was originally the signal to leave), and the burning candle reappeared. This recalled the death ("and the earth did quake, and the rocks rent" (MATT 17:51)) and resurrection of Christ, Light of the World.

Our *Tenebrae* service on Good Friday evening is an adaptation of this ancient practice and consists of two nocturns with the *Benedictus* and final antiphon.

Holy Saturday

This is one of the most ancient festivals of the Church; it is known as the Great Sabbath or the Great Night and is thought to be of apostolic origin.

There is no mass on this day even though the Prayer Book does not forbid a Communion service. It is customary to hold only the Ante-Communion, as was the ancient practice of the Gallican and Ambrosian Churches. The Epistle alludes to the Descent into Hell, a subject of much controversy and discussion in the Church. The collect is from the Scottish Book of 1637 and refers to baptism.

In the early church, the catechumens who were to be baptized during the following night were assembled in the morning or early evening. They were marked with the sign of the cross, the Gospel (Matthew 19:13) was read to them; they were subjected to an exorcism; their ears were symbolically unstopped, their nostrils opened, and they were anointed on the back and breast. They then renounced Satan and the recited the Creed.

The main service of the day is the Great Easter Vigil which lasted all night in the early church. By the twelfth century, the service was anticipated to noon on Saturday and from the fourteenth to mid-twentieth centuries, it was held in early morning. It was restored to the evening by Pius XII in 1951.

The blessing of the fire opens the vigil. This is a Celtic custom dating at least from the times of St. Patrick (d. 461). It is perhaps related to the spring fires of the Druids and was adopted in Rome only in the ninth century. The fire is drawn from a flint, symbolizing Christ's coming out of the stone of the tomb. The five incense grains inserted into the candle symbolize the spices used to embalm Our Lord's body (JOHN 19:40), particularly those put on his five Glorious Wounds.

The use of the Paschal Candle is more widespread. In the time of the Emperor Constantine the Great, a column of wax was erected in church and lights adorned the city to such an extent that night was said to be turned into day. The candle is lit from the newly blessed fire at the church door and carried in procession into the church to the singing of "The Light of Christ."

Up to some thirty years ago,[9] three tapers fixed on a reed trident were first lit and carried in procession. These were then used to light the Paschal Candle in the quire. The candle itself was often too large to be moved. The Paschal Candle of Salisbury Cathedral in 1517 was thirty-six feet high and one is mentioned at Westminster weighing 300 pounds.

By the fourth century, it was the custom to sing a joyful song of Easter (*Præconium paschale*) around it. The *Exsultet*, traditionally sung by a deacon wearing a white dalmatic, recalls the events in marvelous text and music; it is said, without much proof, that the *Exsultet* was composed by St. Augustine, whilst still himself a deacon, or else perhaps by St. Jerome. It is without doubt the most glorious passage in the whole of western liturgical music.

The Prophecies, or Lessons, recalling the beginning of the history of our salvation are then read as a preparation to the baptisms. There were twelve such readings at Rome with collects and canticles in between.

The baptismal ceremony is one of the high points of the Vigil, though it has lost much of its importance with the decline in adult baptisms. But this is changing as we now live in a more secular world and adult converts become more numerous. First the font was solemnly blessed in an elaborate ceremony, involving a procession during which Psalm 42 ("Like as the hart desireth the water-brooks") was sung. This was followed by a long sung preface, a pouring of oil (chrism and oil of cathecumens) into the water, the dunking of the candle into the water (perhaps recalling an ancient fertility

---

[9] The author writes from the year 1989.

rite) and a litany. The catechumens and, with them, the whole congregation, turned to the West to renounce the devil, and then to the East to affirm their faith by saying the Creed. The presentation of a candle to the newly baptized is a Gallican custom. In ancient practice, baptism was followed immediately by confirmation and the new Christian was admitted to Holy Communion. Members of the congregation are then aspersed with the blessed water in remembrance of their own baptism.

The mass starts immediately after the *Kyrie* from the Litany. In Hereford use, as in that of the Gallican Church of Lyon, there was a special hymn *Accendite* ("Light up"), marking the lighting of the church. There are no antiphons for the introit, offertory, and communion, probably because the service antedates the introduction of these songs. There is no exchange of the peace (probably by accident, because the peace was given in early times before the canon during the offertory; it was lost over the years). Some liturgists think the absence of the *Pax* recalls Our Lord's order to Mary "Touch me not" (JOHN 20:17).

Bells are rung throughout the *Gloria*, symbolizing the joy of Easter; the Lenten array is taken down; and the *Alleluia* is solemnly welcomed back three times after the Epistle. The Gospel is sung with incense, but without lights ("when it was yet dark," (JOHN 20:1)). The Creed, already said at the baptisms, is not repeated.

Eastertide

Easter Day

This is the earliest festival celebrated by the Church, and it is mentioned by St. Polycarp of Smyrna, a disciple of St. John. The name *Easter* probably comes from the Old English *oster* ("to rise"), but the Venerable Bede held that it came from *Eostre*, the Saxon goddess of dawn (dayspring) and spring. Other names for the feast include the Pasch, the Uprising of Our Lord, and the Again-rising.

Its date remains a bone of contention among Christians to this day, despite the fact that the first Ecumenical Council at Nicaea in 325 tried to give an unequivocal rule to calculate the date; the Second Vatican Council in an appendix made a plea to all Christians to come to a common understanding on this point. In early times, the date was computed and announced by the Patriarch of Alexandria on Epiphany each year. When Augustine of Canterbury came to Britain in the early seventh century, he found there Celtic and Anglo-Saxon Churches which celebrated Easter on a different day (cycle of Sulpicius Severus) from Roman use (cycle of Victorius Aquitanus), and this led to much discussion and confrontation, which was finally resolved at the Synod of Whitby in 664.

In the Middle Ages the actual date of the first Easter was reckoned to have been March 27 and the date is marked as such in the Celtic Tallaght Martyrology.

In our First Prayer Book (1549), there was a special service to be said before Mattins, consisting of sentences, a versicle, and a collect. This apparently was meant to replace an ancient English custom of going to the Easter Sepulchre where the crucifix and a consecrated Host had been enclosed on Good Friday. Three clerks representing the three Marys and two deacons representing the angels reinacted the scene at the tomb. They carried the Sacrament back to the Altar while singing "Christ rising again from the dead" and the Sacrament was put into the pyx, which was usually in the form of a dove and hung over the High Altar. In the Second Prayer Book (1552), the sentences (with the *Alleluias* removed) were incorporated in Mattins, replacing the *Venite*, and this remains our present practice.

In the early church, the Easter service was that of the Vigil, and the morning mass was added only in the fifth or sixth century. Most of its present texts are from the eighth century. The collect is from the Gelasian Sacramentary, but the ending was altered in the fifth century after the Pelagian heresy to stress the necessity of grace which the Pelagians denied. The Epistle is that of the Vigil and the Gospel was originally prescribed for Easter Saturday. Our first service was the second in the 1549 Prayer Book.

In the evening, the mediæval English church had a procession to the font, commemorating the baptism of the eve. A similar practice was held in Rome at St. John Lateran, which holds Rome's main baptistery.

Eastertide lasts until the eve of Trinity Sunday, fifty-six days. In the new calendars, it ends on Pentecost Day which no longer has an octave, so the "Sacred Fifty Days" are restored. White vestments are used, the gradual is replaced by an *Alleluia* verse, and *Alleluia*s are added to all antiphons and verses. It was an early practice to pray standing instead of kneeling during this time, as prescribed by the Council of Nicaea (325).

The decoration of Easter (Pasch or Paste) eggs is an ancient practice, and Edward I is said to have distributed some in 1307. Eggs were forbidden during Lent, so their return to the table was an occasion of rejoicing. Also, eggs are symbols of the grave and resurrection.

The eating of ham on this day is also a sign of rejoicing, as the pig is a symbol of good fortune. The Pope traditionally eats lamb. Easter-ale was customary brewed and drunk in mediæval Britain. Rabbits and hares were associated with Eostre, the spring goddess, probably as symbols of fertility; they thus also became related to Easter.

It is a universal custom in the Church for the faithful to greet one another on this day by the salution "Christ is risen; he is risen indeed."

The Easter solemnity was celebrated all week (Code of Emperor Theodosius), but was reduced to three days in the Middle Ages, and our Prayer Book provides special services for Monday and Tuesday which are expanded from the Sarum services.

On Wednesday, it is customary for the Pope (on every seventh year of his pontificate) to bless *Agnus Dei*s, which are wax from the previous year's Paschal Candle and from candles left from Candlemas. They are sent to various churches and given to the newly baptized as memorials. Their importation into England was forbidden by Elizabeth I.

On Saturday (*Pascha annotina*) a special commemoration was made of those who had been baptized the previous week and they were invited to renew their baptismal vows.

Octave Day of Easter

Low Sunday

This day in known by many names: Low Sunday (by reference to Easter which is a high Sunday), Close Sunday (marking the end of the festivities), second First Sunday (the first being that after Epiphany), *Quasimodo* Sunday (from the first word of the Sarum introit *Quasimodo geniti infantes*), and Laud Sunday (from the first word in the Sarum sequence, *Laudes Salvatori voce modulemus supplici*).

Our service today follows Sarum use. The *officium* (introit) refers to the newly-baptized as "newborn babes." The Gospel was considerably shortened to take out the scene of the meeting of the resurrected Christ with Thomas, which our Prayer Book reserves for St. Thomas' Day. Before the Reformation, this day was also known as St. Thomas Sunday.

The mass was originally set on Easter Saturday, but was moved to its present place when an Octave Day for Easter was instituted in the seventh century. Modern calendars have the Easter Octave ending on Saturday evening, so this day is now referred to as Easter 2, which is the ancient usage.

Annunciation of the Blessed Virgin Mary

St. Mary's Day in Lent, Lady Day, Conception of Christ, March 25

It appears that the date March 25 was chosen following computations of the accepted date of Christ's death by Christian chronographers in the third century.

For reasons of symmetry and order, it was felt proper that Our Lord should have lived an exact number of years, hence the anniversary of the Incarnation was set on this day also (at midnight). Following the same reasoning, it was held that the Creation of the world, the Fall, Abraham's sacrifice, and the Exodus had all occurred on this day, and that the Last Judgment was also to be expected on a March 25. An alternative hypothesis is that the date was chosen by counting back from Christmas.

And indeed from early times, a parallel was drawn between the world damned through Eve and redeemed through Mary, both on this date (Iraenaeus of Lyon). The feast was celebrated first in the East (5th c.), then in the West (6th–7th c., Pope Sergius). In the Visigothic Church, the feast was on December 18 and called the Expectation of Mary, and to this day the Annunciation is remembered on that date in Spain. Similarly the Roman Church commemorates the Expectation of Mary on Ember Wednesday in Advent.

This day's service is from the Sarum Missal, but we use as the collect the postcommunion of the old service, which beautifully links the Christmas and Easter cycles. The Sarum antiphons are used rather than those from the Roman Missal which are more Marian. Our antiphons are mainly from the Golden Mass (*Rorate cæli*, "Drop down, ye heavens") which in our use is said today, but in Roman use is celebrated on Ember Wednesday in Advent.

From the Norman Conquest in 1066 until 1752, this was New Year's Day in Britain in the Old Style Calendar. "We begin therefore our ... year with the glorious annunciation of his birth by angelical embassage" (Richard Hooker, 1594).

It is significant that the octave of today's feast is April Fool's Day, which has some characteristics of an ancient New Year festival with its rejoicing and tricks (hunting the gowk). The Romans had a feast of *Cerealia* on this day when people were sent on fools' errands. The Jews started the year around this time at the full moon following the spring equinox. This day marked the traditional return date of swallows to Britain.

Rogation Sunday

The Lesser Litanies

In 467 Gaul was rocked by earthquakes, and Mamertus, Bishop of Vienne, prescribed special prayers (rogations) in procession for the three days preceding Ascension Day to plead for God's mercy. These became an annual event during which protection was sought from all disasters, both temporal and spiritual, and now special prayers are offered for the year's harvest. The custom spread to the Gallican (510), Anglican (747), and Roman (c. 800) Churches.

At the Reformation, this was the only procession retained (actually restored by the 1569 Elizabethan Prayer Book); it is also known as "the beating of the bounds," "the perambulation of the parish," and "the riding of the marches." Although the proposed service was not adopted, a homily was provided (*Second Book of Homilies*, Homily 17).

These were "Gang Days" when the clergy, parish officers, and children carried poles decorated with milkworth (gangflower) and willow wands, and went around the parish bounds. Boundary markers were beaten with the willow switches by the choir-boys. Some of the boys were held by the feet and bumped on the boundary markers "to impress on their minds the limitations of the parish so they could testify of boundary stones." Some of the markers were trees, often called Gospel Oaks because the procession stopped and Scripture was read near them.

The custom arose from a similar Roman procession (circumambulation) each spring when the limits of the city and fields were visited and Terminus, the god of boundaries, was honoured.

The mass on this day is that appointed for the Fifth Sunday after Easter. The Gospel is most appropriate. The Rogation Day service was restored in our 1918 Prayer Book, following the proposals of the Savoy Conference (1661), but in 1959 it was replaced by a new service inspired in part by the Sarum Missal.

The Greater Litany was a similar observance instituted in Rome (590) on St. Mark's Day (April 25) superseding the pagan feast of *Robigalia*, to appease Robigus, the god responsible for frost and wheat rust. Our Litany originates from the prayers used on these "Days of Asking."

Ascension Day

Holy Thursday

One of the oldest of Christian festivals, said by Augustine to have been instituted by the Apostles themselves. It concludes the Great Forty Days of Easter, although the Paschal season ends only at the onset of Evensong on the eve of Trinity Sunday.

The collect of the day, from the Gelasian Sacramentary, is very beautiful both in language and substance. The communion verse bids us to look to the East, to the sun rising where Our Lord has disappeared and from whence he will return. This is particularly appropriate in our church, given our eastward position and the reredos depicting the ascending Christ. During the singing of the Gospel, the Paschal Candle, symbol of the earthly presence of the resurrected Lord, is extinguished.

It is customary to eat fowl on this day and to make pastries in the form of birds. The habit of visiting and decorating wells on this day is related to the pagan *Fontanalia*, or feast of the gods of fountains, held at this time of year in ancient Rome.

Sunday after Ascension Day

Expectation Sunday

The mass is taken from the Sarum Missal except the beautiful collect which Cranmer substituted for the rather nondescript mediæval one. The new collect is based on a Sarum antiphon for Vespers ("Leave us not comfortless") which the Venerable Bede recited on his deathbed on Ascension Eve in 735. The ten days between Ascension and Whitsun are called Expectationtide, in remembrance of the Apostles' wait for the gift of the Comforter.

Whitsunday

Day of Pentecost

The Gift of the Spirit to the Apostles on the Jewish festival of Pentecost (fifty days after Passover in commemoration of the gift of the Mosaic Law) is celebrated in this, one of the major feasts of the Christian year. It is therefore the anniversary of the foundation of both Judaism and Christianity.

In the Anglican tradition, it is the White Sunday, a day when new Christians, baptized on the eve during a vigil ceremony similar to that we now have at Easter, adorned the church in their white robes. Baptisms were traditionally performed at this time in Northern Europe instead of at Easter as in Rome, no doubt because of the colder climate.

The service is from the Sarum Missal and contains the beautiful Golden Sequence (c. 1210). This sequence was regarded by Archbishop Trench as the "loveliest hymn ... of sacred Latin poetry" (*England's Book of Praise*, Telford) and is often attributed to Archbishop Stephen Langton (d. 1228) of Magna Carta fame. The collect is from the Sacramentary of Pope Gregory the Great (c. 600). The red vestments recall the "cloven tongues, like as of fire" (ACTS 2:3).

The festival is also known as Rose Sunday (*Pascha rosatum*) since rose petals, symbolizing the tongues of fire, were customarily dropped from the eye of the dome in *Santa Maria Rotonda* (Pantheon) in Rome. The custom was initiated in many mediæval English churches and firebrands were also used. Doves were sometimes liberated in church.

Festivities extended until Wednesday (Council of Constance, 1094), but this was gradually shortened to Monday (Clement XIV, 1771) and to the feast day (Pius X, 1911). Whitsun-ale was traditionally brewed and offerings ("pentecostals" or "Whitsun-farthings") were made to the parish priest.

Summer Ember Days

Ember Days were observed from earliest times in the Roman Church. Callixtus (c. 222) and Leo the Great (c. 450) wrote a series of sermons for these days. They were at first days of fasting in thanksgiving for the harvest and originally there were three Ember periods, one for wheat, one for wine, and one for oil (winter sowing, summer reaping, autumn vintage, according to other interpretations). They were perhaps also inspired by the seasonal days of fasting of the Jews (fourth, fifth, seventh, and tenth months).

They later became associated with the civil year, then (eighth century in England; c. 1080 in Rome) with the church year (Advent, Lent, Whitsunday, but the fall Ember Days are still attached to Holy Cross Day), and at the council of Placentia (1095) were fixed as special days for ordinations in the Western Church. The association of fasting and prayers with ordinations comes from the example of the Apostolic Church (ACTS 6:6).

The Prayer Book did away with the mediæval services appointed for the Wednesdays, Fridays, and Saturdays, but two collects were added in 1662 to be said every day during Ember weeks for the ordinands.

Our Prayer Book (1959) provides a service (collect, Epistle, and Gospel) applicable to all Ember Days, irrespective of season. The collect is taken from the Scottish Prayer Book of 1637. The association with the harvest was soon lost and retained only in the mediæval fall service; the services for the other seasons stressed Christ's coming (winter), penance (spring) and joy (summer). Our services refer to ordinations or to church unity (alternative proper).

The word "ember" derives from the Anglo-Saxon *ymbren* which means *circuit* or *round* and refers to the cycle of the seasons. Others think it derives from cakes baked on embers on these days. The periods are also known as "Quarter Days" and "Quatertemps Weeks."

Trinitytide

From Advent to Trinity, the Church makes us relive the great mysteries of our faith (*credenda*, that which we believe); from Trinity to Advent, we are reminded of the duties and virtues of Christian life (*agenda*, that which we do).

In early missals there were only a few services provided for this period and they were repeated as required. Later, an organized series of masses was set up. Sundays were numbered serially from Trinity (or Pentecost), instead of being grouped around major saints' days (the Apostles, St. Lawrence, and St. Cyprian in some uses; St. John, our Lady, St. Michael, and St. Martin in others).

The liturgy is based on a serial reading and use of Scripture. Generally, the verses (introit, *Alleluia*, offertory, and communion, but not gradual) are taken sequentially from the Psalter.

Similarly, the Epistles are from St. Paul and the portions appointed are in biblical order. The Gospels are mainly from St. Luke and St. Mark, and more or less alternate between parables and miracles.

Trinity Sunday

The addition of Trinity Sunday to the series of great festivals extending from Advent to Whitsunday is of Northern European origin, perhaps even from the Celtic Church. Alcuin, the learned English monk, had composed a votive mass c. 780. Thomas Beckett, who was consecrated on this day in 1162, is largely responsible for its popularity. The feast was belatedly adopted by the Roman Church in 1334 (Pope John XXII) who after much hesitation comissioned John Pecham, future Archbishop of Canterbury, to compose a mass for the occasion. Pope Alexander II had previously (c. 1070) rejected the festival as superfluous since the Trinity is honoured continuously in the doxologies of the liturgy.

Doxologies arose in the Orient in Constantinian times and were added to the psalms by the Council of Narbonne (589). The sign of the cross also recalls the Trinity: at first the sign was traced in silence on the forehead with three fingers.

Our service is that of the Sarum Missal. The last sentence of the collect, altered in 1662, was restored to its original meaning in our Prayer Book, but in a different style. The festival was deemed so important that in Britain (as in Germany, Iceland, and the special rite of the Dominican friars) it became customary to count ordinary Sundays as "after Trinity" instead of as "after Pentecost" as was done in southern Europe. The feast supersedes the original Octave Day of Whitsunday, which is no longer celebrated.

Feast of Corpus Christi

In the Middle Ages, because of an increasing devotion to the Blessed Sacrament, a need was felt for a special feast honouring the "Most Holy Body and Blood of Our Lord." The commemoration of the institution of the Sacrament on Maundy Thursday comes during Holy Week, when we are overwhelmed by the themes of grief and suffering. A special festival was therefore planned for the first available Thursday after the Paschal Season and was celebrated as early as 1208 (1246?) in the diocese of Liège in Belgium under the influence of a saintly nun, Juliana, prioress of Mont-Cornillon Augustinian Convent.

The mass we sing today was commissioned in 1264 by Pope Urban IV, a former archdeacon of Liège, from the greatest theologian of the time, the Dominican friar Thomas Aquinas. This explains the superb architecture of the service, where every text is masterfully chosen and ordered for our edification and devotion. Thomas, the "Angelic Doctor," also uses the occasion for our instruction, and succeeds in the sequence in condensing the mediæval doctrine of the Eucharist (see # 317[10]), which is apparently based on the hymn *Laudes crucis attollamus* of Adam of St. Victor (d. 1192).

By the fourteenth century, mass was traditionally followed by an elaborate and joyful outdoor procession with the pyx (later the Host exposed in a monstrance) offered to the worship of the people, and from this derives our service of Benediction.

The Roman Church had an additional Feast of the Most Precious Blood on the first Sunday of July. This was instituted by Pius IX on his return to Rome after an exile to Gaëta during the 1848 Revolution. It was transferred to July 1 by Pius X and is now joined with Corpus Christi in the new Roman calendar as the Feast of the Holy Sacrament of the Body and Blood of Christ, celebrated on the Sunday next after Trinity.

---

[10] "Laud, O Sion, thy salvation", The English Hymnal (1906)

First Sunday after Trinity

Our Prayer Book follows the Sarum Use, which differs from that of Rome in that the propers are offset by one week and the Gospels are often different.

The service for Trinity 1 is thus the mass formerly used for the Octave Day of Pentecost (Pentecost 1), but with a special Gospel (that of Dives and Lazarus). The Epistle is from St. John and is therefore an exception in the series. The collect is ancient (c. 492).

Trinity 3 & 5

These two services share certain traits. First, the Epistles are taken from St. Peter, and therefore differ from the regular Pauline series of Sundays after Trinity. As the Fourth Sunday has the usual Pauline Epistle, this is perhaps due to a transposition of Epistles between Trinity 4 and 5.

The collects which are from the fifth and sixth centuries ask for peace and quietness and refer no doubt to the difficult times at the fall of the Roman Empire and the barbarian invasions.

Nativity of St. John the Baptist

June 24

St. John the Baptist is the only person apart from Our Lord and our Lady whose earthly birth (*nativitas*) is solemnly celebrated by the Church; in all other instances, it is the death of saints (*dies natalis*, heavenly birth) which is commemorated. This is due to the remarkable events surrounding his birth, as recorded in the Scriptures, particularly to his receiving the Holy Ghost in his mother's womb. His birth is also a major event leading to the Incarnation.

The feast is probably of Western origin, as the Eastern Churches celebrate the Baptist on Epiphany. The date was fixed by reference to St. Luke who places John's birth six months before Our Lord's; the feast is on June 24 and not as expected on June 25, because the dates are from the Roman calendar and both correspond to the eighth day before the Kalends of January and of July respectively.

In mediæval times, the feast was treated as a summer Christmas, to the extent of establishing an Advent-like preparation of four weeks and a special vigil, and celebrating three masses on the feast day. There was also a feast of the Conception of St. John in September, still extant in some Eastern Churches. The death (passion or beheading) of the Baptist is commemorated on August 29.

The feast comes near the summer solstice (the longest day of the year, June 21); liturgical symbolists see in the shortening days which follow the image of the declining of the Old Covenant as they see in Christmas and the increasing day lengths the coming of the New Covenant.

St. John is the secondary patron (since the twelfth century), after our Blessed Saviour, of the Golden Archbasilica, St. John Lateran in Rome, which is the mother church of Western Christianity ("mother and head of all churches," as reads its frontal) and was founded by Constantine the Great in 324. The name was originally given to the adjoining baptistery which was at the time the only one in Rome, and tradition wills that all baptisteries be dedicated to John the Baptist, and many, as our own, contain a prominent picture of him baptizing Our Lord.

The mass is taken from the Sarum Missal, except the Epistle and the collect, which was composed in 1549 for the First Prayer Book. The Gospel was expanded to include the *Benedictus*.

Early French settlers in Québec brought with them the mediæval custom of celebrating Midsummer's Eve (*La nuit de la Saint Jean*) by building on hills large bonfires blessed by the bishop or the priest, but this practice gradually disappeared after the conquest. In 1834, Ludger Duvernay, a founder of the *Société Saint Jean-Baptiste*, chose this day as a National Day for French Canadians (perhaps under Masonic influence) and Pius X (1907) declared St. John patron of French Canada. It is the National Feast Day of Québec. St. John is also patron of Newfoundland and of our Canadian Church.

Today is also the anniversary of the first recorded Church of England service on the mainland of the North American continent by the Rev. Francis Fletcher in 1579 near what is now San Francisco.

St. John was the patron of the eleventh-century Order of St. John of Jerusalem, dedicated to the care of the sick and the wounded during the Crusades. It became a military order in the twelfth century with a mission to guard the Holy Land and its pilgrims. It inspired the nineteenth-century creation of the St. John Ambulance Brigade.

St. Peter & St. Paul

The Apostles' Day, June 29

From the earliest times, the commemorations of the two major apostles have been linked, since they both ended their ministry in Rome and suffered their martyrdom there, supposedly on the same day (February 22, June 29 or August 1 in the year 63, 64, 66 or 67, according to various conflicting traditions). The feast was first dedicated to all apostles and is the oldest of saints' days. June 29 is perhaps the anniversary of the translation of the relics of the Apostles.

Since the service for June 29 was centred around Peter, a special commemoration of Paul was celebrated on June 30, beginning in the times of Gregory the Great (c. 600). The true reason may have been that it was not convenient for the Pope to celebrate mass at both places of martyrdom of the Apostles on the same day, given the distance between the two shrines, St. Peter's on Vatican Hill and St. Paul's Without in Ostia.

Our Reformers reduced the feast to St. Peter's Day (St. Paul being commemorated on January 25, the Conversion of St. Paul). The association of both saints was happily restored in our 1959 Prayer Book. The service contains the collect for St. Peter from the 1549 Prayer Book, an additional collect for St. Paul, a new Epistle and the Gospel and other propers from the Sarum Missal, but the emphasis remains on St. Peter. A second service is offered for the Octave which gives a more balanced commemoration.

The new Roman calendar has a joint feast for Peter and Paul on June 29 and a Commemoration of Early Roman Martyrs on June 30.

Visitation of the Blessed Virgin to Elizabeth

July 2

This is a late mediæval feast (1389 in Rome), originating with the Franciscans and particularly St. Bonaventure, which came to be accepted in Britain only in 1480. It was placed on July 2 as the first day available after the Octave of St. John the Baptist, instead of in its logical place near Lady Day (Annunciation, March 25) where it would have interfered with the numerous liturgical commemorations at that time of the year. York held it on April 2.

It was instituted in Rome to ask for celestial help during the Great Western Schism (1379–1417) when up to three popes reigned simultaneously. In the new Roman calendar the feast is celebrated on May 31.

It is also the Day of the Hallowing of St. John the Baptist in his Mother's Womb and the Day of the *Magnificat*.

Lammas Day

St. Peter's Chains, St. Peter in Fetters, August 1

The mediæval service for this day was of Roman origin and commemorated the dedication of a church to St. Peter and St. Paul in the fourth century. The church received precious relics from Empress Eudoxia, the fetters supposedly used to tie St. Peter when he was jailed by Herod in Jerusalem, and the church was renamed St. Peter *ad Vincula* (5th c.). The feast replaced the traditional festival in honour of Augustus Caesar for whom the month is named.

The most famous of Anglican churches dedicated to St. Peter *ad Vincula* is no doubt a chapel in the Tower of London, in which lie "the Duke of Somerset and the Duke of Northumberland between Queen Anne and Queen Katherine (also Lady Jane Grey), all beheaded."

Lammas Day (*hlam-masse*, "loaf-mass"), celebrated on the same day, was dropped from the First Prayer Book (1549), but was restored in the Second (1552) as a black letter day. In the early English Church, it was a custom to offer loaves made from the first corn ("the first-fruits of wheat") in thanksgiving in years when the harvest was good. The feast is superseded by our Thanksgiving festival in October. The term *lamb-mass* was also used, and in some places lamb tithing was practiced, a reference to Peter's mission to "feed my lambs" (JOHN 21:15). This was also a quarter-day, on which Peter's Pence was paid.

Transfiguration of Our Lord

August 6

The manifestation of Our Lord's divinity to three of his apostles—Peter, James, and John—is celebrated in this ancient festival of the Church. It is of considerable importance and solemnity in the Eastern Churches. It replaced a feast of the goddess Diana (Feast of the Flowers) celebrated in pagan times on the same day. It was extended to the Western Church in 1457 by Callixtus III to commemorate a victory over the Turks near Belgrade by the Hungarian John Hunyady, on the previous year on this date.

Our Reformers left it out of the Calendar for no apparent reason since it passes both the criteria of ancient prescription—though celebrated in Britain only since 1480—and scriptural warrant; perhaps they wished to restrict the number of holy days during harvest time. The feast was restored in our 1918 Prayer Book, following the American example of 1886.

The propers are from the Sarum Missal, except the collect which is adapted from the American Book.

On this day new grapes are blessed; it is the *Jour des raisins* in France and *Liebfraumilchtag* in the Mosel region of Germany. At Tours, grapes were squeezed into the consecrated chalice at mass.

Most Sweet Name of Jesus

August 7

This is a festival which had long been celebrated in the English mediæval church on January 1. No reason is known for its transfer to August 7.

In the Roman Church it was popularized by the Franciscan (grey) friars, in particular St. Bernardine of Sienna and St. John Capistrano in the fifteenth century, but was not of universal acceptance before 1721 (on the second Sunday after Epiphany). It is now celebrated on January 2, or the Sunday between New Year's Day and Epiphany in the Roman calendar. It is a feast of devotional origin and does not integrate well in the regular church year.

With this feast is associated the beautiful mediæval hymn *Jesu, dulcis memoria* (# 238[11]), often ascribed to St. Bernard, Benedictine abbot of Clairvaux ("The Song of the Blessed Bernard ... concerning the Most Sweet Jesus," as it was then known), but it is probably anterior to him.

Our Prayer Book fittingly uses the service of the Octave Day of Christmas with a special collect.

Falling Asleep of the Blessed Virgin Mary

The Assumption, The Virgin's Repose, Our Lady in Harvest, August 15

This has been from early times in both the Western and the Eastern Churches a major festival honouring our Lady. Celebrated at first on January 18 in Gallican use (Our Lady in January), it was transferred to its present date under the Eastern Emperor Mauricius, c. 602, but this was not immediately accepted, particularly in Northern Europe.

Unfortunately our Reformers took the feast out of the calendar in 1549 because it did not stand the test of Scripture, at least regarding the tradition of the bodily Assumption, although it passed that of antiquity, being mentioned in the fourth century at the Council of Chalcedon. It was restored in

---

[11] "Jesu! The very thought is sweet", The English Hymnal (1906)

our 1959 Prayer Book as a black letter day, without a special service and is now acknowledged as a holy day in the Book of Alternative Services (1985).

On the Octave, August 22, used to be celebrated the Feast of the Blessed Heart of Mary; the new Roman calendar contains the feast of St. Mary the Queen. There was also in France a Feast of the Joys of our Lady celebrated on the Sunday within the Octave.

It is not known whether our Lady died in Jerusalem or in Ephesus where St. John lived. There is an ancient (at least fifth-century) and widespread tradition in the Church that she was taken body and soul into heaven at her death. The Roman Church declared this an article of faith in 1950 (Pius XII, *Munificentissimus Deus*).

The Sarum service exalted the role and dignity of the Mother of God, but it is in no way comparable to the remarkable service written by Pius XII, in which Mary appears under the images of the "the woman clothed with the sun" of Revelation, Judith saving her people by her courage, "the woman bruising the serpents head" of Genesis, and the beloved of the Song of Solomon.

During the French regime in Canada, this was an important holiday since Louis XIII had consecrated his kingdoms to Mary in 1638 and pledged an annual evening procession after Vespers in her honour. In some churches, it was customary to bless flowers, fruits of the harvest, and other plants remarkable for their nourishing and medicinal properties.

In mediæval England, people bathed in the sea, lakes or rivers for what they called "our Lady's health bath." In Portugal and in the United States, fleets are blessed on this day.

Nativity of the Blessed Virgin Mary

September 8

Nine months after the Conception of Mary (observed on December 8), the Church celebrates this festival of the birth of our Lady. The feast comes to us from the East, where it arose c. 450, perhaps as a dedication memorial of a now-forgotten church, possibly in Jerusalem on the supposed site of the house of Joachim and Anne. The Western Church did not adopt it before the eighth century and the feast did not become universal before the twelfth century when it was popularized from the great shrine of Our Lady of Chartres in France.

In southern Europe, it is a feast of the wine harvest and, in mountainous areas, it is the day when flocks return to the lowlands. Fields and seeds are traditionally blessed. Swallows were said to leave for the tropics on this day.

The Sunday following used to be dedicated to the Holy Name of Mary, a feast of Spanish origin (1513) extended to the Western Church by Innocent XI in thanksgiving for the victory of John Sobieski of Poland over the Turks near Vienna in 1683.

Holy Cross Day

Holy Rood Day, Roodmas Day, September 14

In the mediæval church there were two festivals honouring the Holy Cross.

The earlier, the Invention of the Holy Cross on May 3, commemorated the discovery of Our Lord's Cross by Helena, the mother of Constantine, and the dedication of the churches of the Holy Sepulchre and of Calvary in Jerusalem in 335 on the sites of the Passion, known as the Martyrium. Calvary had been enclosed since 135 in the Roman city of Aelia Capitolina, and bore temples to Jupiter, Juno, and Venus. Part of the relic of the True Cross was kept in Jerusalem, part in Rome, where a basilica was built to house it (*Santa Croce in Gerusalemme*), and part in Constantinople.

The second feast, the Exaltation of the Holy Cross on September 14, recalled the solemn return of the relic to Jerusalem by Emperor Heraclius in 629, after it had been taken by the Persians in 614, and the dedication of a new basilica encompassing the two earlier churches. The Jerusalem relic disappeared in 1187 when Saladin pillaged the city.

Following the Reformation, the two feasts were combined and references to the relics were removed. The service is that from Passion Sunday with a special collect. Until 1840, the Jews of Rome were compelled to go to church on this day and hear a sermon. The practice was abolished by Gregory XIV.

On the Octave Day, the Roman Church celebrates a second Feast of Our Lady of Sorrows, instituted by Pius VII in 1814 as a thanksgiving for his return from exile in France where he was prisoner of Napoleon Bonaparte. Our Lady of Sorrows is also remembered on Friday of Passion Week.

Autumn Ember Days

The Autumn Ember Days originate from the custom in the early church of fasting and praying during the pagan *Vinalia* (festival of the grape harvest) held at this time in ancient Rome. This harvest festival has been replaced by our Thanksgiving.

Since Gelasius (c. 494), Ember Days are devoted to praying for the ordinands who are about to receive Holy Orders and for vocations in the Church. However, each seasonal Ember Week is given a particular secondary theme in our Prayer Book. Fittingly, in autumn, thanksgiving is given for the labour and industry of men and women in our society and a special service (1959) is therefore provided.

Trinity 18

Vacant Sunday

This Sunday originally followed the Autumn Ember Week. However, the date of the Autumn Ember Days is now attached to Holy Cross Day and the Sunday has become detached from them.

Since the evening celebrations on Ember Saturday usually lasted until the next morning, there was no service provided for Sunday, hence the name. When Ember Day services were transferred to the Saturday morning, the void on the Sunday was filled by using a service originally created for the dedication of a Roman Basilica to St. Michael. As its themes are the House of God and the Second Coming, the mass is quite appropriate for this time of the Christian year.

The collect is an expansion by Cranmer of an old Roman collect from the Sacramentary of Gelasius; the propers and Epistle are from the Sarum Missal; the Gospel is new.

St. Michael & All Angels

Michaelmas, The Heavenly Virtues, September 29

The feast originally commemorated the dedication in 530 of a basilica which no longer exists on the *Via Salaria* near Rome to St. Michael and all angels. Michael, whose name means "Who is like God?", is the best-known and most-often-mentioned archangel in Scripture. Traditionally, he is considered the champion of the Church. It is he who is said to lead the souls of the departed into paradise.

Before the Reformation, there were at least two other feasts of St. Michael in the calendar, both recalling apparitions: on Monte Gargano (492) in Italy on May 8 (St. Michael in the spring) and on Mont Tombe (8th c.), now the site of the famous Benedictine Abbey of *Mont St. Michel* in Normandy, on October 16. A similar vision was reported on an island near Land's End on the Cornish Coast in 495; the site became known as St. Michael's Mount and was an important pilgrimage centre in the Middle Ages. In 1044, Edward the Confessor gave the island "for the salvation of (his) soul" to the black monks (Benedictines) who built an abbey there. There were also chapels dedicated to St. Michael on Glastonbury Tor and Brent Tor.

Another famous site dedicated to St. Michael is *Castel Sant'Angelo* in Rome on the Tiber in front of the Vatican; the fortress had been built as Hadrian's tomb in 138. In 590, during a plague, after public prayers ordered by Gregory the Great, Michael was seen on the pinnacle putting his sword back into his scabbard, thus ending the plague.

The Roman Church has additional commemorations of guardian angels on October 2 (Clement XV, 1672), and of Gabriel on March 24 and Raphael on October 24 (both Benedict XV, 1921). The Eastern Churches celebrate the Synaxis ("rallying") of St. Michael and all Angels on November 8. All these feasts are combined in today's festival.

The original mass is now used for Vacant Sunday (see above). The service we sing today is a mass formerly in honour of guardian angels (Ps 91:11). The collect is from the Sacramentary of Gregory (c. 590), the Epistle from the ancient feast on October 16, and the Gospel and the propers are from the Sarum Missal.

In England, Michaelmas is a legal quarter-day. "The Michaelmass goose is the roast proper to the feast," no doubt because the fowl is fat and abundant at this time of year during its southward migration.

Dedication Festival

Although all churches are dedicated to God and to his worship, it is customary in naming a church to honour a special attribute of God, an event of the history of our salvation, or the memory of a saint. The Celtic Church even thus honoured the founder of a particular church.

The Convocation of 1536 began the practice in the Anglican Church of commemorating the consecration of churches on the first Sunday of October, irrespective of the actual consecration date. Our church was consecrated June 4, 1905, by Archbishop Bond; it had been dedicated on March 6, 1878.

The practice of havng an annual commemoration of the dedication of the Temple was observed in the Old Testament, and is still part of the festival of Hannukah. In Early Christian times, Sozomen (5th c.) reports celebrations on the anniversaries of the dedication of the Constantinian basilicas of Jerusalem.

The Roman Church celebrates the dedications of the four Major Basilicas, that of St. Mary Major (Our Lady of the Snows) on August 5, that of St. John Lateran on November 9, and that of St. Peter Vatican and St. Paul Without on November 18.

In many churches, a second festival is celebrated on the feast day of the patron, the Patronal Festival or Feast of Title. Ours is on May 6, the Feast of St. John *ante Portam Latinam* (St. John at the Latin Gate), a feast now absent from most calendars, including the Roman and our own. It is traditional for churches dedicated to St. John to choose the May date instead of the December one because of the latter's proximity to Christmas.

The propers are from the mass written for the dedication of the Roman Pantheon by Pope Boniface IV in 610. The collect is from our 1919 Church Consecration service, minus the last sentence; it is originally from the Scottish Book of

1912 and was adapted by Bishop Dowden from the Gregorian Sacramentary. The readings are from the Scottish Prayer Book.

Thanksgiving

The original thanksgiving day in the English Church was Lammas Day (August 1) when firstfruits were offered. There was a similar festival on Martinmas (November 11). Thanksgiving as we know it is a North American festival. It was apparently celebrated as early as 1578 in Baffin Land by Martin Frobisher and his crew.

Its celebration on the second Monday of October is peculiar to Canada. Our 1959 Prayer Book provided a special service for the day. The antiphons and verses in this day's mass are taken from the Votive Mass of the Blessed Sacrament.

St. Simon the Zealot & St. Jude, Apostles

with St. Jude the Brother of Our Lord, October 28

This feast was originally of Simon and Jude, associated probably because they occur together in the Gospel list of Apostles. However, the name Jude or Judas has led to some confusion. It was assumed for a long time that the apostle Jude or Thaddaeus was the same as the Jude who wrote the Epistle. It is now understood that it is another Jude, called in the Gospel Judas, brother of Our Lord (and therefore also brother of James), who is the author of the Epistle.

Our 1959 Prayer Book took this into consideration by naming both Judes. The service is from the Sarum Missal, except for the collect which was written by Cranmer (1549), the supplementary collect for the Brethren of the Lord (1959), and the Epistle, most appropriately from the Letter of Jude (the only use of this book in our liturgy of the mass).

All Saints' Day

All Hallows' Mass, November 1

This was originally a festival on May 1, commemorating the transformation of the dome-like Pantheon (a temple in Rome dedicated in 27 BC by Marcus Agrippa to all gods—hence its name—and restored by Hadrian but unused since the early fifth century) into a Christian church honouring Mary and all Martyrs. This was done by Pope Boniface IV in 610, on May 13, the feast day of "the Martyrs of the whole world," a festival celebrated in Edessa as early as 373. A similar feast is mentioned as early as 270 by Gregory the Wonderworker.

The building was covered with gold leaf and bronze and was one of the most splendid in Christendom. It housed twenty-eight cartloads of relics of martyrs excavated from the catacombs. It was pillaged by the Goths and repeatly vandalized for construction materials and metals till the Renaissance, but it still is in use under the name *Santa Maria Rotonda*.

In 732, Gregory III dedicated a chapel in the Old St. Peter's Vatican to Mary and all Saints and the feast lost its restriction solely to martyrs. Its general celebration on November 1 in the Western Church dates from 834 by order of Gregory IV and Emperor Louis I the Pious. The transfer of the feast to November is perhaps related to the fact that it was easier to feed the crowds of pilgrims attracted to Rome for this festival in the fall after the harvest than in the spring. On the other hand, November 1, being the Kalends of November, was also the first day of winter, and it was appropriate that the season be marked by a great feast; it was also New Year's Day in the Celtic calendar. The Eastern Church has a similar commemoration on the Octave Day of Pentecost.

Our Reformers retained the feast and gave it prominence because it replaced the innumerable saints' days stricken from the calendar. The mass is from the Sarum Missal and was written in the ninth century. Cranmer wrote a beautiful collect stressing the Mystical Body and hence the Communion of Saints.

It was a custom in many orders and areas to hold a special festival during the octave commemorating all the local saints or the saints of the order. Our 1959 Prayer Book, following the 1928 Deposited Book of the Church of England, has revived this practice and proposes a special service for the Octave Day in which the "unnamed saints" of our Canadian church are remembered.

The practice of Halloween has no Christian connection and is related to the Druid festival that was celebrated at this time in honour of Saman, the god of death. It was the last day of the year in the Celtic calendar. It was sometimes called Nutcracker Eve when nuts were eaten in thanksgiving to Pomone, the Roman goddess of fruits, for the gifts of apples and nuts.

All Souls' Day

November 2

Having honoured on November 1 the Church Triumphant, the mediæval church now remembered the Church Suffering, "those who still long in purgatory," in the words of the Martyrology, and offered prayers so that "they may quickly attain to the fellowship of the heavenly citizens."

Our Reformers, in reaction to abuses of their time, adopted the Protestant doctrine that the souls are now at rest, rejected as non-scriptural the existence of purgatory and the efficacy of prayers for the dead, and struck this commemoration from our calendar in 1552. Likewise, all direct prayers for the dead were removed from our liturgy. This, thought our Reformers, was the practice of the Early Church.

More careful scholarship, however, shows that the early Christians did indeed pray for the dead, particularly on the third, seventh, and thirtieth days after death and on anniversaries. St. Augustine (c. 420) reminds the faithful of their duty to pray for the departed, especially for those who have no remaining family or friends, so that they not be deprived of prayers. However, no general commemoration was celebrated, probably to counter the then prevalent rituals of ancestor worship, particularly the *Cara cognatio*, or loving-remembrance festival (February 22), of the Romans.

Some churches started in the fifth century to commemorate the departed on Maundy Thursday, but the practice was frowned upon (Council of Braga in 563). It is only in 998 that Odilo, the Abbot of the famed Benedictine Abbey of Cluny in France, introduced the custom of reciting the *Placebo* (Vespers from the Office for the Dead) after the Vespers of All Hallows, singing the *Dirige* (Mattins and Lauds, hence our "dirge"), and celebrating requiem masses on the morrow in commemoration of all the faithful departed.

From Spain came the custom for each priest to celebrate three propitiatory masses on this day and this was generalized in the Roman Church by Benedict XV (*Incruentum altaris*, 1915), perhaps as a substitute for foundation masses and chantries. In Catholic countries, the people usually took time off work in the morning to participate in the masses, and so apply the merits gained to the faithful departed.

Anglicans, as firm believers in the Communion of Saints, continued the practice of remembering their beloved departed before God in their prayers. After the carnage of the First World War, the need for formal prayers grew considerably, and it was felt that our Church should resume the practices of the Church catholic. Our 1959 Prayer Book finally provided a special service for All Souls' (following the examples of the Depsited Book of the Church of England of 1928 and the Scottish Prayer Book of 1929). The collect and Gospel are new, and the Epistle is from an old Common of Martyrs. The

Book of Alternative Services recently repopularized direct intercessions.

The custom in our own church is to celebrate morning and evening masses and to pray for the repose of the souls of the parish, especially for those remembered in a special list drawn up for the occasion. In many places, it was customary for the people to hold lighted tapers during mass to symbolise the souls of the departed. Similarly, in Latin countries candles are lit in graveyards.

Feast of Christ the King

Sunday next before Advent

This is a recent feast celebrating the kingship of Our Lord in this world, instituted by Pope Pius XI in his encyclical *Quas Primas* in 1925 and adopted by many churches besides the Roman. It was originally celebrated on the last Sunday of October, but has now been transferred to the last Sunday of the Christian year, the Sunday next before Advent.

Some Protestant churches have the feast on the last Sunday of August where it marks the beginning of Kingdomtide, the last segment of the church year (for them the last Sunday of October is Reformation Sunday, commemorating Luther's posting of his Theses in 1517).

Our service today is the Roman mass created in 1925 which makes use of the royal psalms (2, 29). The collect is a variation on the Roman collect and the readings are new. As an alternative, we also use the collect and the readings from the Advent Ember Service which have peace as their theme.

The original intent of the feast was to stress the spirituality of the world, and to condemn the secularism, materialism, modernism, and liberalism of our present society. It is to be a reparation for the general apostasy of nations. The devotion to

Christ the King as such figures prominently in the spirituality of some conservative groups, such as the Roman Catholic breakaway group led by the late Archbishop Lefebvre.

It replaces in our use the Sunday next before Advent which develops a pre-Advent theme. It contains its original collect of the Advent "*Excita* (Stir up)" series, which generations of schoolchildren have deformed into the well-known petition "Stir up, we beseech thee, the pudding in the pot," hence the name Stir-Up or Pudding Sunday.

Bibliography

The information in these notes has been gleaned from a variety of sources, the main ones listed below. It can in no wise be taken as a critical account, but efforts were made to obtain confirmation from both Anglican and Roman Catholic sources when possible.

Aigrain, R. *Liturgia* (Paris: Blond et Gay, 1930).

Anon. *Helps to the Study of the Book of Common Prayer* (Oxford: Clarendon Press, c. 1890).

Cabrol, F., Leclercq, H., and Marrou, H. *Dictionnaire d'archéologie chrétienne et de liturgie* (Letouzey et Ané, 1907-1953, 30 vols).

Daniel, E. *The Prayer-Book. Its History, Language, and Contents* (London: Wells, Gardner, Darton & Co., 1913).

Dix, G. *The Shape of the Liturgy* (London: Adam & Charles Black, 1945).

Gibson, G.M. *The Story of the Christian Year* (Freeport NY: Books for Libraries Press).

Guéranger, P. *L'année liturgique* (Tours: Mame, 1841... , 15 vols).

Hole, C. *English Custom and Usage* (London: B.T. Batsford, 1944).

Martimort, A.G. *L'église en prière* (Paris: Desclée et Cie, 1961).

Parsch, P. *Le guide dans l'année liturgique* (Mulhouse: Salvator, 1935... , 5 vols).

Procter, F. and Frere, W.H. *A New History of the Book of Common Prayer* (London: Macmillan, 1905).

Shepherd, M. H., Jr. *The Oxford American Prayer Book Commentary* (New York: Oxford University Press, 1950).

Urlin, E. L. *Festivals, Holy Days, and Saints' Days* (London: Simpkin, Marshall, Hamilton, Kent & Co., 1915).

Wheatly, C. *A Rational Illustration of the Book of Common Prayer of the Church of England* (London: Knapton et al., 1729).

About the Author

Born in Masson, Quebec on September 4, 1942, Peter Harper died at home in Saint-Hubert, Quebec on April 29, 2019. During his nearly seventy-seven years, he lived a rich and rewarding personal and professional life. Along with his family, the abiding passions of his life were biological research, specifically entomology, and religion.

Educated at Collège Saint-Alexandre, Gatineau, and Université Laval, where he earned a BA in Classical Studies, Peter's original intention was to become a missionary priest in Africa. During the course of studying for a BSC ('66) in biology at Université de Montréal, his life changed course when he met Françoise Delorme, a fellow student. In 1967 they each earned an MSC in biology. They married and went to the University of Waterloo, where Françoise gave birth to their daughter, Catherine, and Peter earned his PH.D ('77). After one year of postdoctoral study in France they returned home, and Peter embarked upon a career as professor in the Department of Biological Sciences at Université de Montréal, publishing over one hundred papers—some co-authored with Françoise. Peter retired in 2004 and cared for Françoise, who had developed Parkinson's disease; she died the following year.

Along with science and family, religion served as a lifelong bond between Peter and Françoise. Born, raised, and educated as Roman Catholics, they became discouraged with the liturgical and theological changes accompanying and following upon the Second Vatican Council (1962–1965). Looking for an acceptable alternative, in the late 1970s they began attending the Church of St. John the Evangelist in Montreal, whose traditional Anglo-Catholic theology and liturgy alongside liberal social attitudes appealed to them.

Françoise, with her musical sense and fine alto voice, became a member of the choir. Peter became enthralled with the history of St. John's and its relationship with the Anglo-Catholic movement and Christianity's Western Rite tradition. He earned a series of theological degrees at McGill University (BA '93) and Université de Sherbrooke (Certificate '03 and MA '13). As chair of St. John's Music and Liturgy Committee and through his authorship of numerous booklets and studies of St. John's, he played an important role in determining the parish's direction on liturgical and theological issues. His work as the parish historian, although unfinished, has provided an enduring memorial to the important role of the Church of St. John the Evangelist as the Mother Church of Canadian Anglo-Catholicism.

Peter F. McNally, The Church of St. John the Evangelist

Printed in Great Britain
by Amazon